What Mothers Are Saying About *Flex Appeal*

"*Flex Appeal* helped me put many of my feelings into perspective. I felt empowered and that I had the knowledge and the right to seek out a flexible work arrangement."

Erin, sales manager

"*Flex Appeal* inspired me to think about what I really want to do. It also alleviated my fear and without fear anything seems possible."

Lorie, stay-at-home mom and former recruiter

"I'm impressed. This is a very well-written, organized book with a great mix of personal stories and constructive suggestions."

Suzanne, book publishing executive

"This book will not only inspire you to make the change, it will show you how and remind you that you are worth it!"

Rosemary, media promoter

"I think many of us know intuitively what we need to do; it's the motivation we need. I liked the pep-talk aspect of *Flex Appeal*. It made me feel like I should take control of my work situation."

Marta, journalist

Flex Appeal

AN INSPIRATIONAL GUIDE TO FLEXIBLE WORK FOR MOTHERS

Jacqueline Foley

Out of Our
Minds Press

The material in this publication is provided for information purposes only. This book is sold with the understanding that neither the author nor the publisher is engaged in rendering legal, accounting or other professional advice. If expert assistance is required, the service of a competent professional person should be sought.

National Library of Canada Cataloguing in Publication Data

Foley, Jacqueline, 1965–

Flex appeal : an inspirational guide to flexible work for mothers

ISBN 0-9689932-0-6

1. Working mothers. 2. Hours of labor, Flexible. 3. Part-time employment. I. Title.

HD6055.F64 2002 331.4'4 C2002-900099-8

Cover photo by Peter Bregg
Cover design by Dakis & Associates
Text design by Kim Monteforte, Heidy Lawrance Associates

Printed and bound in Canada

Published in Canada by
Out of Our Minds Press
158 Church Street
Stouffville, Ontario
L4A 4T6

To my firstborn Zachary for inspiring me to find a better balance and to my husband Vince for believing anything is possible.

Contents

HOW TO GET THE FLEXIBLE WORK ARRANGEMENT YOU WANT

FLEX APPEAL RESOURCES

Foreword

I'm not the first woman to think I could have it all. I believed I could raise my children with all the hands-on attention I felt good parenting required, and have a career at the same time. Then came the days of mixing and matching schedules that defied my imagination, and I wondered if I'd live to tell the tale. Five a.m. hockey practices didn't exactly match up with 9:00 a.m. editorial meetings. Writing assignments in far-flung parts of the world had to be scheduled around piano recitals and parent-teacher meetings. Midnight trips to the grocery store, where I invariably met all my friends who were equally time-challenged, became a bizarre part of my routine.

We were the generation that ventured en masse into the workplace. We were going to have our careers and our families. But we ran smack into the Super Mom Syndrome. Our consolation was that we would bring down the barriers and change the workplace so that our daughters would be free to follow their stars, raise their babies and fulfill their career ambitions. It didn't happen. Today's young moms feel just as harassed and overwhelmed as we did.

Jacqueline Foley decided to do something about this. Soon after her son Zachary was born, she took a long hard look at the business she was running with her husband and at the miracle of life they had created together as parents. Then she crossed North America talking to women who found themselves in the same situation. And she came up with a prescription for their modern-day malaise. Parenting can and should be a joyful time, a time to grow. Keeping up with a career or the job that helps make house payments needs to be part of that growth. But how can an overworked, frazzled mom do both? Foley presents the solution in *Flex Appeal.*

Foley writes like a mentor to millions of North American moms who could use an experienced guide to walk them through the peaks and pitfalls of balancing work and kids. She addresses the issues at hand: How important is career advancement to you? How much risk can you take? Is job sharing for you? She gives a step-by-step guide for staying connected at home and at work and for coping with predictable objections from your boss. *Flex Appeal* is all you ever need to know about keeping your sanity and taking control of your life. It's an intelligent look at the realities in women's lives and a soothing reminder that you really can have the best of both worlds.

Sally Armstrong

An award-winning journalist and human-rights activist, Sally Armstrong is editor-at-large at Chatelaine *magazine and a contributing editor at* Maclean's *magazine. Sally lives just outside of Toronto, and is the mother of three grown children.*

INTRODUCTION

Why Women Yearn for Flex Appeal

The idea for this book was born soon after my first son, Zachary. While I had always thought of myself as a career woman, having a child changed my perspective completely. Becoming a mother made me look beyond how much money I made, how quickly I grew my consulting business or whether others saw me as successful. Zachary opened my eyes to the sheer joy of being a mom and living in the moment with him – whether it was sharing a warm, sleepy cuddle after his afternoon nap, or seeing the scrunched-up look on his face as he tasted his first solid food. Within weeks of having Zachary, I knew I needed a balance between the work I enjoyed and the son I loved. And this balance could only come from changing the way I worked and lived my life.

Thinking about working a more flexible and reduced schedule challenged me to the core. I was terrified of taking a step back and losing the momentum I had built over a ten-year career. I couldn't imagine how I would continue running the business my husband and I shared on a less-than-full-time basis. But then again, I couldn't imagine not being with my little Zachary.

How my personal journey became a book

I was a woman on a mission, trying to figure out how to create the right blend of work time and Zachary time. I pored over books, websites, and newspaper and magazine articles, looking for any shred of advice or inspiration that might lead me down the right path. While I found helpful bits and pieces of information, there was no one comprehensive guide to flexible work, especially one geared to moms.

That's when I turned to other women. I accosted moms in coffee shops, at parties and at my son's playgroup. I called complete strangers I had read about in the media or been referred to by friends, colleagues – even my hairdresser. Overall, I spoke with more than 100 mothers across North America who had made the transition from full time to a flexible work arrangement to gain more time with their children. Somewhere around my 25th conversation, I began to see a compelling need for a book that would bring these women's stories and the many lessons that they had learned to other moms. Here was an opportunity to develop an invaluable tool for those wanting alternative work options – the kind of tool that I could have used myself.

What you will find in this book

When I set out to write this book, I was determined to avoid the pitfalls of many of the books I had read on work/family balance. For starters, you won't find any annoying tips on how to multitask better, like the book that suggested I clean the bathroom while my children are taking a bath. I believe women are looking for more time to enjoy their kids, not how to fit even more tasks into what little time they have. You also won't find any miracle solutions or magic cures for the challenges you are facing. They simply don't exist.

You will find inspiring stories of women who have successfully and happily shifted to flexible work, along with the real-life trade-offs they have made and the challenges they have faced. This book is practical, too. First, it will help you determine whether flexible work makes sense for you. Then it will help you create your own personal vision of work/family balance. Finally, it will help you translate that vision into a flexible work arrangement that is right for you and your family. There's a step-by-step process to help you get the flexible work arrangement of your dreams – from having a plan to preparing a proposal and pitching it to your boss. And you'll learn about what to expect after you make the shift to flexible work and how to make the most of it.

Who should read this book

Just about any mother, or mother-to-be, can benefit from reading this book. It doesn't really matter how old your children are. If you feel like you need to change the way you work to have more time with them, then read on. Mothers who are already working flexible hours can also benefit from this book. You can read about what other women are doing and gain insights from their experiences. You may also find it validating to learn that you are not alone in facing the conflicting emotions and challenges that come with shifting to a flexible work arrangement. I certainly did.

What I hope you get from this book

My journey toward a better work/family balance eventually led me to a three-day workweek, and it's been a wild and wonderful ride. Sure, there have been trade-offs, such as earning less money, moving out of the city, and scaling back on my business plans, but it has been well worth it. I really do feel I am living the best of both worlds. And that is my hope for you, too: that this book will inspire and help you to make changes in your life that bring you better balance. From one mother to another, I encourage you to listen to the women in this book and go after what you want.

CHAPTER 1

What They Don't Teach You in Prenatal Classes

"If I hadn't had my son, I wouldn't be working as a part-time aerobics instructor today. I always wanted to teach more and get rid of the administrative part of my job, but I was afraid I wouldn't make enough money. Having children made me realize that you have to trust your gut and listen to what it is saying you really want to do. Then you need to have the confidence to try something different."

Tiffany, mother to Tyler, four, Jessica, two, and Abby, two months, traded in a fitness management position to work as a part-time aerobics instructor.

Thinking back to those last few hours of life as I knew it before children, I realize now that I was completely unsuspecting, even delusional. I mean there I was wrapping up a client meeting and, though I was quite sure I was already in labor, I heard myself promising to e-mail her something by the next week. Clearly, I had absolutely no clue how having a baby was going to change my life.

Don't get me wrong: On many fronts I knew what to expect. I had a pretty good picture in my mind of what giving birth was going to be like and – thanks to many videos and forthright mothers – how painful and messy the whole ordeal was going to be. I had learned the important skill of getting the baby to latch onto my nipples even before I had a baby to practice with. I was armed with critical new-mother tidbits, such as how to hold my newborn's head and what to do when my little baby came down with a cold or fever. But nowhere in the books I read, the videos I watched or the prenatal classes I attended did they warn me about the biggest challenge I would face as a new mother: How would I ever make a place for this little baby in my already busy, work-consumed life?

All of a sudden the career I had devoted most of my waking hours to before the baby became a distant second to the sweet-smelling little creature cooing in my arms. I know I'm not alone here. So many women I've met and spoken with suffered the same shock and complete shift in priorities when their first baby (or second or third) came into the world. And I suspect if you've picked up this book, you know what I'm referring to. Or you are about to find out!

Becoming a mother changes everything

Like so many women of my generation, I always considered myself fortunate to have grown up with a women-can-do-anything mentality. Knowing that women of prior generations had paved the way for me to do great things, I took this responsibility seriously and envisioned a successful career for myself. Though I always planned to have children, I guess I never really thought about where they would be while I was busy being successful. Even when I got pregnant, I never second-guessed my vision for my life. I was a brand-new partner in a consulting business with my husband, and I had great plans for its growth.

Then nine-pound, three-ounce Zachary popped into my world and turned it completely upside down and all around. It's not that I didn't expect to fall in love with my new baby, but I never imagined just how hard I would fall. Within weeks of Zachary opening his eyes, I became consumed by every little sound and movement he made. I felt like I was in the throes of a new romance. The more I got to know Zachary, the more I wanted to be with him, getting to know everything I could about him. I was intoxicated by his new-to-the-world smell, his coy smiles and the way he snuggled sleepily into my neck after he ate. I was especially addicted to his wide open-mouth kisses.

After years of being wrapped up in our work, we feel funny when it doesn't seem so almighty important anymore. Yet on the other hand, we are terrified of what this means.

The transformation I went through in having Zachary was more monumental than any I had experienced in all my 32 years. Zachary became my catalyst for making important changes to my life, changes that have made me a far happier and more relaxed person today. He challenged everything I had ever held dear, especially how I felt about my work. All of a sudden, my pre-Zachary focus of wanting to grow my business seemed to melt away like ice cream on a hot summer day. The notion of work paled in comparison to the monumental responsibility of nurturing and guiding my baby's life. His was an exciting new world that I wanted desperately to take part in.

Struggling to come to terms with my new emotions and rapidly changing priorities, I had to work hard at accepting that I simply didn't care as much about my work as I did before the baby arrived. I found myself asking: Who am I? So many women I have spoken with struggled with this issue, too. After years of being wrapped up in our work, we feel funny when it doesn't seem so almighty important anymore. And yet on the other hand, we are terrified of what this means. We ask ourselves: Have we lost our ambition? Are we becoming our mothers? (Sorry, Mom.) Were we just fooling ourselves all these years in believing we wanted to be equal to men in the workplace? The answer to all these questions, of course, is no. But we can't expect to be the same women we were before we had kids. We have gone through a major metamorphosis, one that is now challenging us to figure out exactly how we will balance our need to mother with our need to work.

Facing the most difficult decision of your life

I knew instinctively as I gazed down into Zachary's six-week-old eyes that I couldn't possibly go back to full-time work. I needed quantity time with Zachary to have quality moments. I knew that I could never get enough quantity within my existing work arrangement. On the other hand, I couldn't possibly imagine becoming a stay-at-home mom and giving up my work completely. After all, while I didn't feel as strongly about work as I did before I had Zachary, I was also realistic about the fact that I needed to work for my own sanity and self-worth. Truth be told, I wasn't prepared to give up my entire income either.

This is often the crossroads at which most new mothers and mothers of young children find themselves. Most of us need the income to support our growing families. And let's face it, deep down we aren't really excited about giving up the many other important benefits that working brings, such as feelings of accomplishment, social contact with other adults, mental stimulation and so much more. At the same time, we can't stand the thought of spending too much time away from the little bundles of energy who have captured our hearts and our focus.

The bright side is that we've come a long way from the tough decision women used to face: to work or not to work. At least we have other options that allow us to do something in between full-time work and no work at all. There are women working every kind of flexible work arrangement imaginable, whether it's job sharing, working a reduced number of days per week or telecommuting. Women are successfully finding the right mix of mommy time and work time. They are getting the best of both worlds, and so can you.

Why flexible work could be the answer

A flexible work arrangement is a great way to secure some quality time with your children, while keeping one foot on the career or job track. There is simply no better way to be a mom, while keeping your professional skills up-to-date and earning an income. And if you do it right, you can literally create a customized solution to fit the kind of life you want to live. If you want Fridays off to take your new baby to a mom-and-tot group, you may find working a four-day week is right for you. If you want to be near your children so they can come and tell you a story or get a hug, you may find that working out of your home is the answer.

When I first made the shift to a flexible work arrangement, I was driven by two things: wanting Zachary to spend more time with me than with another caregiver, and needing enough days in the office to stay connected to my work and my clients. When I first went back, I worked three days a week. After the first year, my husband muscled in on one of my days with Zachary (okay, maybe muscled in is a bit strong: he is his father, after all). As a result, we shifted to each having one day a week with Zachary – he got Mondays, I got Fridays – and working the other four. Finally, when Zachary started going to preschool three mornings a week, we reduced our caregiver's days to two a week and I basically juggled my work schedule around his school schedule. Many of my friends and family members are amazed at how I have been able to switch back and forth between work and Zachary throughout the day. For me, it's about being able to take time out with Zachary when I want to, so I'll do whatever it takes to achieve that goal.

In speaking with more than 100 women across North America about how they managed to find balance through flexible work, I was struck by the number of different arrangements that women had created for themselves. The possibilities are truly endless. One mother of two quit her job as a travel agent to make specialty chocolate baskets out of her home. A single mother left a high profile publicity job to start her own publishing company. Numerous women, including a public health nurse, a communications consultant and a fraud investigator, successfully convinced their employers to let them restructure their jobs to accommodate their children. One woman even walked into her boss's office planning to quit but ended up negotiating a part-time workweek from home, scheduled completely around her daughters' changing needs.

Flexible work arrangements give moms the opportunity to attend a school play or go to the park on a sunny day.

The bottom line is that flexible work arrangements give moms the opportunity to attend school plays, go to the park on sunny days or stay home without guilt when their children are sick. So it's no surprise that moms who are doing it just love it. They feel a lot more balanced, and less stressed and harried. Women report having more of a sense of control over their time, even though they still have work obligations, deadlines to meet and coworkers or clients to deal with. For me, having the flexibility to do errands like grocery shopping on weekdays means that weekends are devoted to fun activities with Zachary and not running around like a maniac. And there's nothing like waking up on a Friday morning to Zachary crawling into my bed and asking: "So, Mom, what do you want to do today?"

Another important reason for considering a flexible work arrangement is that it's good for our sanity. Our work is an important part of our identity. We need to remember that we are women first and mothers second, although I know it usually feels like the other way around. I believe it's very important to nurture our other parts, the ones that aren't necessarily connected to being a mom. Even though being a mother can be an incredibly rewarding role, many of us need more in our lives. We need our work because it gives us a different sense of accomplishment and pride, and it challenges us in ways that being a mom can't. We need adult time, too.

Then there's the money. We shouldn't underestimate how valued we feel when we are contributing to our household income. While flexible work almost always requires a reduction in income, it still allows us to get paid for the work we do. Many of the women I interviewed for this book found that taking a pay reduction of 20 or 40 percent wasn't completely unmanageable, especially given the tremendous benefits it brought them – more time with their kids. And even though they had reduced their annual income, the 60 or 80 percent that they were still bringing home was very important to them and their families.

Battling the fear of change

While there are clearly some incredible benefits to working a flexible schedule, you will no doubt be fraught with fear at the thought of taking a step in this new direction. Don't let the fear of failure get the best of you. You need to ignore those irritating voices of self-doubt that we all hear when we're considering making a change to our lives. My little voice used to badger me with: You don't really think you can have a successful business working three days a week? Good thing I didn't listen, because today I am running a business I consider successful and continuing to work flexible hours.

Here are some of the doubts you may experience:

I can't afford it

While this may be true, how will you know until you actually give some serious thought to what kind of arrangement or budget might work for you? You need to be clear about what family and personal goals you are trying to achieve, and only then can you begin figuring out what kind of flexibility makes sense and what that will mean financially. Chapter 2 will help you develop your vision and work through how you might afford it. Even if it appears at first like it can't be done, don't give up until you've explored every angle. It would be a shame to let money deter you before you even get started.

My job doesn't lend itself to a part-time schedule

Not every job can be redesigned to suit a flexible work arrangement, but many can. Pat Brown, vice president in charge of

First Tennessee Bank's workplace flexibility initiatives, believes almost anything can work if you put your mind to it. She encourages women to think outside the box and to be creative if they want to make a flexible work arrangement a reality. The trick is to find a balance between your needs and what makes sense for the kind of work you do. For instance, if you're an administrative assistant and you spend a lot of time interacting with your boss and other people in your department, three days a week might be an option, but working from home may not. Or if you think you'd like to job share, you need a role that allows you to split up tasks between two people easily; otherwise you'll end up working overtime with the other person just to get projects completed. Chapter 3 will help you figure out your own Flex Appeal Profile and what kind of flex arrangement might suit your situation.

My supervisor will never go for it

How do you know your supervisor won't go for it if you haven't pitched it to her yet? I know it feels like a big risk, but you'll never know unless you try. You simply need to take the time to prepare. You need a plan and a written proposal so you can show her you've really thought it through. Chapter 4 will help you design your proposal and Chapter 5 offers tips on how to actually pitch it to your boss. Most of the women I know who took the time to put together a thoughtful plan found their bosses very receptive and, in many cases, very impressed with the work they had put into it.

This could really limit my career

Many women worry about how their request to change to flexible hours will be perceived by the people they work with.

Specifically they are concerned about being branded as less committed and losing out on opportunities for promotions and advancement within their companies. The reality is that people will likely see and treat you differently if you shift to a flexible work arrangement, but it's up to you to show them that you're still as committed as before. Chapter 6 will give you some great pointers on how to balance your need for recognition and career advancement with your desire to work more flexible hours.

I'm still going to go crazy trying to juggle work and kids

Juggling is never easy, no matter what your situation. Many women, however, are amazed at how working only a few hours less a week can make all the difference in achieving a better work/family balance. Only you can determine what that right balance is, and realistically you can't really know until you're doing it. Of course, even the best flexible work arrangement won't ensure a perfect balance; you have to be willing to really work at it. Chapter 7 offers practical advice on how to do just that.

What it takes to make the transition to flexible work

So what does it take to get some Flex Appeal in your life? You've got to want it more than anything. Jim Freer, vice chair of human resources at Ernst & Young, agrees. "You have to have a commitment that what you're doing is right, deep in your heart," he says. "If you're in halfway, it won't work." Making the transition to a flexible work arrangement takes time and energy, and it can be stressful. Having said that, the benefits are great and, as most women would agree, well worth the effort.

Ask yourself: Am I willing to put my all into this? You need to be prepared to take the time to re-evaluate your life and develop a new vision for your future. Once you have a vision, it takes planning to figure out exactly how to rework your job or skills into a new flexible work arrangement. Then you must sell your boss on what you want and be ready to really work at it when he says yes. Or you may have to rethink your strategy if he says no, whether that means starting your own business or changing companies.

Achieving your vision requires taking risks and stepping out of your comfort zone. In many ways, it's like trying to find your way through a foreign city without a map. When you set out, you really have no idea where you'll end up. So you need to trust your instincts and have faith in your ability to reach your destination. You have to be willing to stop and ask directions if you get lost. And above all, you must be prepared to take a few detours along the way. These are all things that women in flexible work arrangements experience at one time or another.

Nothing in life comes without compromise – at least nothing this good.

Opting for a flexible work arrangement almost always requires trade-offs. Nothing in life comes without compromise – at least nothing this good. You may have to give up a percentage of your annual income, especially if you're looking to reduce your hours. Your career aspirations will likely have to be readjusted in some way. Slowing down the amount of work you do often equates to a slower climb up the career ladder. Perhaps you don't want to put your children in day care, but in the end this may end up being the only option available if you're determined to work a flexible schedule. Getting more time with your children may require these and other trade-offs, so be prepared.

Good things come to those who act

Here is your chance to carve your own path – one that allows you to continue working while taking pleasure in the joys of motherhood. It has worked for me and for the numerous women who have shared their stories in this book. And with a little (okay, maybe a lot) of determination and by following the steps in this book, it could work for you, too.

Ready. Set. Go!

CHAPTER 2

Out with the Old, In with a New Vision

"Since I've made the shift to part-time work, I am personally happier. I have more time to do things with my children, things that aren't just about getting 'through the routine.' Sure I've given up having a bigger house and putting money into savings, but I feel more connected to my kids and generally less burned out. It's been hugely rewarding."

Dana works part time as a journalist and is the mother of Stewart, eight, and Grace, five.

When Zachary was ten months old, I signed us up for a mom-and-baby class. Every Friday morning, we went to the local library to sing songs and play instruments while parading around the room. I learned a lot about Zachary in those classes. Most of all I just loved participating in the activities with him. It was one of the many rewards of having a vision and going after it.

Getting there wasn't always easy. Initially the thought of switching to a more flexible work arrangement made me queasy. I remember getting that sick feeling in the pit of my stomach on more than a few occasions as I struggled to make the right decision for me and my new little baby. You'll likely feel it, too. Don't worry. As soon as you get a clearer understanding of what you're trying to achieve for yourself, your worry spasms will likely subside (or at least become tolerable).

If you're like me, you've probably spent much of your life living out a script that you wrote for yourself years ago. Maybe you've become comfortable earning a certain salary, living in a particular neighborhood or having a title on your business card you worked hard for. But now you're determined to play an active role in your child's life, so you need to make the changes that will help you do that.

If you really want to create something different, you need to dream a little.

This is your opportunity to rewrite your script, to create a new vision for a life that will enable you to balance your work and all of the incredible moments that being a mom will bring. You can build in special times like sharing a picnic with your children in the backyard, looking at ants together through a magnifying glass or catching snowflakes on your tongues. Whatever your vision, the most important thing is to design it to reflect what's right for you and what will make you happy.

Start dreaming

In some ways designing your own vision should be like a brainstorming exercise. Brainstorming is the practice of coming up with ideas or solutions to a problem without ruling out any of the possibilities at the beginning.

When I do visioning sessions with my clients, I encourage them to imagine what their organizations could be like in five years, without factoring in what they can afford or other potential limitations. If you really want to create something different, you need to let yourself dream a little. Maybe your dream is to work out of your home so you can pick up your child from school at 3:30 p.m., or so you can drop your baby off at day care at 10:00 a.m. Or maybe you envision going into work three days a week, so that you can sign up for a new mother's group or a music program at the local library on your days off. Think back to what you envisioned life would be like for you and your new baby back when you were pregnant (or even before you became pregnant). That is, of course, assuming you were able to actually think beyond the incredible impending pain of labor!

Remember, you can always modify the dream when you start factoring in practical realities later on in the process. Many women become so excited about their new vision that they are motivated to find ways to make the vision a reality – even if it initially seems unrealistic.

Reva is one of these women. A 52-year-old author and motivational speaker, Reva was working full time as a conference planner at a university when she had her son, Jonathan, in 1983. Her vision for herself was to return to work part time, but she couldn't get the hours and days she wanted. So she decided to quit her job and focus more seriously on a sideline business she was already running: training people to make presentations, write résumés and develop interview skills.

When her son was 18 months old, she became a single parent and sole income earner (she received no child support). Reva continued to run her own business because she was committed to having the flexibility to be with Jonathan as much as possible. She took big risks to make it work. She asked clients to move seminar times so she could drop off her son at day care. She negotiated bringing her son to out-of-town conferences. She even turned down professional development opportunities because it would have meant too much time away from Jonathan. As a result, she was able to arrange a schedule that allowed her to pick him up from day care at 4:00 p.m. every day. When her business was slow, she took days off to be with him. Once he started school, she participated in field trips and other school activities.

Now that Jonathan is 17, Reva looks back and feels good about the choices she made along the way. And clearly her son does, too. When asked to write an essay in Grade 5 about his hero, he wrote about his mom. He said she was his hero because she ran her own business in order to spend more time with him. Reva says that this was when she first began to understand the positive impact of her choices on Jonathan.

If you already have a very clear picture of the kind of work arrangement you want to create, or think you can figure it out by talking it through with your husband or a friend, go for it! If you're like most of us and you need some guidance through the brainstorming process, this chapter will help you think more concretely about what might work for you and your family. It will walk you through ten key questions you need to ask yourself in order to design a vision for your new flexible work arrangement. Don't worry about taking notes yet; just start trying to connect with what might be right for you. When you're ready to get more serious, you can refer to the more detailed visioning exercise included at the back of this book (page 149).

Remember as you're answering each question try not to think about money until the very end. Money is a means to an end. You have to figure out what kind of end you want for yourself first. Trust your intuition – that powerful gut feeling you get when contemplating whether a change will be right for you. When it comes to making decisions that involve or impact their children, most women have no trouble hearing what their intuition is saying. They just sometimes forget to listen.

Ten Questions to Help Create Your New Vision

I know what you're thinking. You're hoping this visioning thing isn't going to take a lot of time. Maybe you already know you want to work three or four days a week, or you want to start your own business. The only thing I can tell you is if you really want to be successful at creating a more flexible work arrangement, you need specific goals and a plan. Having a plan will help to reduce the stress you are feeling about making changes to your current work arrangement. Developing a clear understanding of what you're trying to achieve for yourself and what your boundaries are will also put you in a better negotiating position when you go in to pitch your plan to your supervisor or your partner or clients.

Your vision is your handprint on life and should be unique to what's right for you.

Question #1: What kind of child care do you envision for your child(ren)?

Most of us don't really know exactly how much time will satisfy our need to be a nurturer, mentor and playmate to our children. But we usually do have a better feel for how we want our children to be cared for. This is the place I suggest women start in designing their visions. Most women have pretty strong feelings about whether they want to be the sole caregivers to their children or whether they're open to other alternatives like day care, relatives or a babysitter.

If your mother, mother-in-law or sister is willing to care for your baby three days a week, then that's probably a good place to start when planning your new work schedule. If you're not fortunate enough to have a relative you can turn to (and most of us aren't), then ask yourself: What can I live with in terms of child care? Some women find that investigating the kinds of day care available in their neighborhood gives them a better idea of their options and their comfort levels with each option. You may want to consider doing this work up front, too.

Vince and I knew right away, within weeks of having Zachary, that we wanted to be our son's primary caregivers. For me this translated into having Zachary spend a minimum of four days a week with us, and not more than three days with another caregiver. We initially planned to send Zachary to an in-home day care on those days. But when we started to envision what we really wanted for him and for us, we decided to hire a caregiver who would come into our home.

This was a difficult decision because it meant spending a lot more money than we had budgeted. But we needed the flexibility of having someone come early and stay late to cover our client meetings. We also wanted the comfort of having both our child and his caregiver nearby. So we paid for convenience and, in the end, peace of mind. Any mother will tell you that you don't want to scrimp on peace of mind. Being comfortable with your child-care arrangement is the single most important factor in being able to focus and enjoy your work.

If you can't envision having anyone else care for your children, then be prepared to reduce your work hours significantly. Of the women I spoke with, most who are their children's only caregivers have been successful at stretching out their work over a five-day workweek and on weekends. This allows them to work when their children are in bed or in school programs, and when their husbands are around.

Thirty-five-year-old Melissa has made this kind or arrangement work for her family. Mother of two sons – Julien, four, and Declan, 11 months – Melissa is the coowner of a video and film production company she runs with her husband. For more than four years, Melissa has managed to work and be a primary caregiver to her two boys. When she first had Julien, she couldn't bear to leave him with anyone else. At the time, she and her husband had been doing freelance video editing and writing contracts. They soon realized that if they took over the production part of the projects, they could make more money and have more control over their time. So they launched their own production firm and four years later, Melissa continues to work around her children's schedules: in the morning before they get up, during nap times, at night when they're in bed and on weekends when her husband can take over.

Question #2: What kind of support can you count on from your partner?

Before you can effectively design your new work schedule, you need to get your partner's buy-in. His support now and throughout your transition to a flexible work arrangement will be critical to your long-term success. Be open and honest, so he can see how important this is to you. Then make sure you have a frank discussion about how, together, you're going to handle child-care responsibilities once you are working a more flexible schedule.

Ask your partner how much of a role he wants to play – and realistically thinks he can – in caring for your children and in helping you work a more flexible schedule. If he has some flexibility with his job, you may be able to count on him to take care of the children when you have to go into the office on an unscheduled work day. Or he may be able to commit to taking over at 6:00 p.m. two or three days a week so that you can work through the evenings after spending the days with your children. Understanding these possibilities and limitations will help you as you think through what kind of arrangement might work for you and your family.

There are so many possible permutations and combinations when it comes to flexible work arrangements. Before you actually take any steps to make your vision more concrete, you and your partner need to explore how you might work together to achieve it.

Question #3: How much or how little do you want to work?

Figuring out how much or how little you want to work may be difficult since you've probably always worked full time. The only rule of thumb I can give you is: The more you feel that your children are a priority over work, the less you should probably plan to work (maybe two or three days a week). On the other hand, if you're committed to building your career, but still want more time with your child than a five-day workweek affords, then four days a week or a compressed workweek might suit you better. The trick is to tap into how important work really is to you and how much of it you're willing to let go to accommodate your new role as a mother.

The trick is to tap into how important work really is to you.

Next you should look at what's realistic for your situation and the type of work you currently do. Ask yourself: How many hours a week do you need to work to stay connected to your job and your colleagues? Tiffany, the part-time aerobics instructor and mother of three, finds that teaching two days a week plus a couple of night classes is enough to keep her in shape and ensure that she maintains a regular following of students. I, on the other hand, am constantly working on projects that require quite a bit of interaction with my clients by phone, e-mail and face-to-face meetings. I don't think I could be successful if I put in any less than three days a week.

Question #4: What hours would you like to work?

One of the biggest benefits of a flexible schedule is being able to work at times that suit the ages of your children and their programs or activities. Think about what hours of the day you want to be available to your children and then what time of day makes the most sense for working. Don't forget to factor in your own productivity. If you do your best work in the early hours of the morning, working from 7:00 p.m. to 11:00 p.m. at night may not be the best idea.

If your children are in school, you may want to be home at 3:30 p.m. every day to talk to them and help them with their homework. If you have a toddler who naps every afternoon, you may want to have time in the mornings to spend with her. Or if you're like me and you work best when you're completely focused, you may want to work three days in a row rather than one day on, one day off. This ensures that the time you get with your child is focused, concentrated time, too. You may find it helpful to make a list of the things you envision yourself doing with your children – taking them swimming, going for walks in the neighborhood or having lunch together. This may give you a feel for what time of the day and what days of the week you want to be available to them.

Donna was working as a director of public affairs for a large hospital when she had her first child, Gabrielle (now two years old). She returned to work after a six-month maternity leave just when her hospital was in the middle of a major merger. Her workload intensified and for eight months she worked at a frenetic pace, coming home two to three nights a week at seven or eight o'clock. Some days she didn't even see her daughter.

Eventually she left the hospital to start her own communications consulting business out of her home. In deciding how to structure her work and her time with Gabrielle, she thought back to what she had liked least about the job she had just left. It was rushing out like a madwoman every morning to get to work. So she made a commitment to herself that she would start work at 10:00 a.m. every day. This way she, her husband (who also runs a business out of their home) and their daughter are able to spend the first part of their day together, going for walks and hanging out at a local coffee shop.

Question #5: Where do you see yourself working?

The answer to this question is usually driven by whether you're an office person or a home office person. Of course, what's possible in terms of your current business or job is important, too. But first you need to understand what kind of work environment is right for you. I've done both – run my business from an office and from my home – and it's like night and day.

When you're in an office environment, there are usually people around to socialize and talk with about work issues. At home, there's you and your computer. Many mothers I spoke with really like getting dressed in "office clothes" a few days a week and going into a professional environment, when the rest of the week they're home playing with dolls or Legos. I've had days when I never got dressed or even had a shower because I popped into my home office and got so focused on my work I didn't quit until 6:00 p.m. When you go to an office you leave your child behind and can actually concentrate on your work. You can feel like an adult, in an adult world. If you're in a home office and your child will be cared for in your house, then you have to imagine whether you can be disciplined enough to work when your child is crying outside your office door.

Moving your office into your home could give you more flexibility than you ever imagined possible. You can do crazy things like roll out of bed at 5:30 a.m., make a cup of coffee and finish a proposal that's due to your client at 9:00 that morning. You can take 15 minutes to give your child a hug when he's not feeling well or listen to the story about the big digger he saw dumping mud on your neighbor's lawn. You can make whatever you feel like for lunch (assuming you have food in the house) and throw in a load of laundry as you're going to do some filing in the basement. The benefits are many. But you have to be disciplined, because there will always be other things you could be doing, such as your grocery list, cleaning that out-of-control drawer in the kitchen or stenciling the bathroom wall. You get the picture.

Question #6: How much flexibility can your job accommodate?

You may be starting to form a picture in your mind of what kind of balance is right for you. Before you make any decisions, you need to test your vision against reality. There are many occupations and positions that require more time than a two-day week, and some that require too much face-to-face contact with clients or coworkers to work from home. You need to think realistically about how your line of work or business can accommodate your emerging vision for balancing work and time with your children.

If you're already running your own business, the first thing you need to think about is whether you can delegate some of the work to a partner or staff person, or hire someone new. If not, you'll need to consider whether your business can survive if you take on fewer projects and are in the office less than five days a week. If you're an employee thinking about working a part-time or reduced workload, can you envision managing most of your current responsibilities when you're not in the office five days? Which responsibilities could be reassigned?

A friend of mine was expecting her second child and contemplating going from a five-day to a four-day workweek. When I asked her if there were things she was currently doing that could be reassigned to someone else (preferably someone at a lower salary level), she estimated that at least 20 percent of her job was making appointments over the phone. She felt this could easily be handled by an administrative assistant. Before she left on maternity leave, I suggested that she start tracking her hours. That way, she could present her boss with an actual breakdown of her duties, specifically showing how to reassign 20 percent of her time to end up with a four-day workweek.

Maybe you're in a job that doesn't require a great deal of interaction with people and could be done at odd hours of the day. Thirty-two-year-old Cathy, an investigator for a government agency that provides legal assistance to people who can't afford it, negotiated to work flexible hours out of her home after the birth of her first son, Dalton. Her job requires assessing lawyers' billings and investigating cases that she suspects are fraudulent.

Since this mostly involves data analysis, she has managed to be a full-time caregiver to Dalton, now two. She works out of her home during his naps, at night and on weekends. Her mother pinch-hits for her as a caregiver when Cathy has to meet with her supervisor.

Question #7: What kind of workload will you be able to handle?

The biggest pitfall for women shifting to a more flexible work schedule is trying to squeeze a full-time job into part-time hours. To avoid this, you need to answer two key questions: How will you reduce your actual workload (or handle it within more flexible hours)? What level of responsibility will you be able to manage within that flexible schedule?

The biggest pitfall for women shifting to flexible work is squeezing a full-time job into part-time hours.

The best way to work this out is to actually list all of your duties and responsibilities and then figure out which ones you can see still carrying out, given the new flexible work arrangement you're envisioning. For instance, you may have been responsible for managing other employees. Can you still effectively manage these people if you work from home? Perhaps you currently manage a sizeable budget. Can you still do this if you work three days a week and won't be signing off on all the expenses? Maybe certain clients are used to dealing with you directly. Have you thought through what they will do on your day off?

Make sure that you paint a realistic picture for yourself because your success depends on envisioning a work arrangement that will make sense for both you and your employer.

Question #8: How far are you willing to commute to work?

For most women working outside the home, commuting is a way of life. I spoke with women who spend up to three hours a day commuting from their homes to their jobs – and this may be you. Now that you have a baby and are looking to spend more time at home with her, you need to think seriously about how far you're willing to travel each day. Even one extra hour a day with your child may make a meaningful difference in how you feel about your time together.

If you really love your job or the company you work for and you plan to be in the office only three days a week, then long hours spent on the road may not be an issue for you. But if the commute was wearing you down even before you had the baby, try to imagine whether you'll be able to manage now that you will be getting your child ready for day care or to be dropped off with a relative or babysitter.

Working out of your home is another great way of cutting down or eliminating your commute because you don't have to rush out every morning. Except for the days when I have to go downtown to meet a client, I find my mornings quite relaxed. Zachary and I get to have breakfast together and play a bit before I have to go into my home office – which is usually at about 8:30.

Question #9: Are you prepared to make a job or career change?

If you are having difficulty coming up with a way to make your current job more flexible, you may need to consider leaving and starting fresh somewhere else. Most companies are still warming up to the idea of flexible work. You may find it's an uphill battle to convince your company or supervisor to support what you're trying to do. But make sure you do your research and put together a thoughtful proposal for your employer before you give up (this will be covered in Chapter 4). Many women assume that because their company does not have formal policies in place or does not have a history of providing flexible work opportunities, that they won't be open to it. This is not always the case. Sometimes it takes a valued employee to change the way a company has traditionally operated.

Forty-two-year-old Eliza decided that she wanted more time with her two daughters, Athena and Amanda, when they were four and two. A computer programmer for an insurance company, Eliza had resumed working full time after her first daughter was born. She began to feel that her daughters were growing up without her and made the decision to carve out more time with them. She knew of no part-time or flex hours in her department and assumed that her supervisor would not be open to it. So she actually went so far as to quit, even though she didn't really want to stay at home full time.

As soon as she told her supervisor her plans to leave the company, he did everything in his power to help her create a work arrangement that would better suit her desire to be with her young children. She eventually negotiated a part-time work schedule spread over five days. She worked primarily from home where she could be the sole caregiver for her daughters, squeezing in work while they were asleep. Looking back, Eliza believes that because she was truly committed to having more time with her daughters – committed enough to walk out the company door – her employer was open to creating the kind of flexible work arrangement she really wanted.

If you don't feel that your company will be the right environment for you now that you have a baby, or if your boss has been unresponsive to your need to create a more flexible schedule, you may need to go somewhere else to find what you're looking for. While there are some resources to help direct you toward a more flex-friendly company, it will take investigation on your part to find a place and a position that are more suited to your skills and offer the kind of flexible work opportunity you're looking for (this is covered in more detail in Chapter 5).

Question #10: What can you afford?

This is the true test of your "visioning" process – whether you can find a way to afford the life you want. Congratulations, you've made it this far! Some women never even make it through the "visioning" part because they convince themselves that they won't be able to afford to work differently. The unfortunate reality is that there are women who really can't afford to reduce their income even by 10 or 20 percent. My hope is that you are in a position to make your vision real, even if it means modifying your income to make it work. Here's how.

The true test of your "visioning" process is whether you can find a way to afford the life you want.

There's no question that more women need to work today to support their families. But it is also true that many of us are in the position to make choices for ourselves when it comes to where we live, what kind of house we live in, how many cars we drive, where we shop for our clothes, whether we bring our lunch to work or buy it and so on. So when many of us say that we can't afford to give up part of our salary, we're often saying that if we gave it up, we would have to change the way we live.

I read about a family that cut their annual expenses by $10,000 in order to work fewer hours and have more time with their children. For six months, they recorded absolutely everything they spent and looked for specific areas to cut back. Mostly they stopped spending money on obvious things, including magazine subscriptions, clothes and eating out. But the thing that struck me was the amount of money they were spending on coffee every day, before they cut back. Both parents worked downtown in a big city and each was buying an average of three coffees a day. This was costing them about $120 a month or $1,440 a year. The couple had to make $3,000 in gross earnings a year just to pay for their coffee habit!

If you want to work less, you're going to have to take a cut in pay. It's that simple. Only about 5 percent of the women I spoke to had actually increased their income since they started working more flexible hours. The other 95 percent had taken a cut, anywhere from a fifth to half of their original income. And guess what? All of these women had to change their spending habits to accommodate this reduction in household income.

As soon as Vince and I decided that I would work three days a week and be with Zachary the other two, it didn't take an accountant to figure out that our total annual income would go down at least 20 percent. At the time we were renting a centrally located, two-bedroom apartment in a large city, and we had a separate office down the street. We had two cars (although his was on its last legs) and we bought our coffee and lunches out every day of the week. Our modest apartment building was located in an upscale neighborhood. As a result, we ended up paying a lot more for dry cleaning, parking, convenience foods and restaurants.

We knew we could not reduce our income and still keep spending at our current level. So we made some major life changes for ourselves and our family. We bought a house in a small town in the country and moved our office into our home. When Vince's car died days before we moved out of the city, we didn't replace it. Now all the money we used to spend on apartment and office rents and Vince's car goes into our mortgage, taxes and paying down the debt we accumulated while I was on maternity leave. Working at home and living in the country saves us a lot of money: Most services are less expensive than in the city.

You may not be prepared to move to a small town to accommodate your desire to spend more time with your children, but perhaps there are other ways that you can curb spending to allow you to realize your vision. Start by making a list of *all* your monthly expenses – from video rentals to alcohol – anything that eats up your income every month. Target the small things and see if you can reduce enough of your spending here to make your new budget work. If not, you may need to look at how you can reduce something more significant, such as your mortgage (can you move to a smaller house or less expensive neighborhood?), car expenses (can you buy a second-hand vehicle?) or groceries (can you shop at a bulk discount store and avoid convenience outlets?).

Remind yourself why you're doing this. Then remind yourself again.

That wasn't so bad, was it? Remember, it's natural when you're developing a new vision to feel a mix of excitement and anxiety. The thing that kept me sane (and I use that term loosely) throughout my own transition to a more flexible work arrangement was keeping my eye on the ball. In my case, the ball was Zachary. When you find yourself panicking about how you'll pay the rent or mortgage, or what this will do to your career, just think about your children. Don't lose sight of them for a minute. They are the reason you started down this road in the first place and they are the reason that you will be thankful that you persevered.

I found it helpful to focus on a particular memory whenever I started getting the jitters about the changes I was contemplating. I was absolutely terrified about moving out of the city to the country (my friends were in shock, too). So I would think back to a morning Zachary and I spent together at a local park. He was seven months old. We lay on our blanket for what seemed like hours, looking up at the trees and the rustling leaves, with him cooing incessantly at the birds and bumblebees. It was one of those "time stood still" experiences I could see us re-creating over and over again once we moved to the country.

CHAPTER 3

Designing Your New Work Arrangement

"We are sold a bill of goods when it comes to the working world. We are told 'it is like this,' and yet there is a world of possibilities out there. I live by the ocean on the east coast of Canada and I can send a file to someone I'm working with in Pakistan. If you only want to work three days a week, then find something that allows you to do it. If you don't want to travel because you'll be away from your child, then say so. Don't put it off. The joys are immense."

Cynthia, a single mother who lives with her four-year-old daughter, Aubrey, is enjoying the flexibility of running her own publishing company.

So you've got a vision or at least some notion of how you'd like life to be different from now on. Don't worry if your vision is as foggy as your bathroom mirror after a long hot shower. It doesn't need to be crystal clear at this point.

Take our decision to move to the country. It did not happen overnight. When Vince and I were trying to envision what would be right for us (a nice way of describing our disagreements), we were at a stalemate on where we were going to live.

For years, Vince had dreamed of moving to the country and having a big stone house on acres of land (this sounded like Ireland to me!). During one of our visioning sessions, I told him I was way too young to retire. He was not amused. What I wanted (or at least thought I wanted at the time) was to buy a house in the city with a third floor that could be made into an office. I wanted to stay in my comfort zone, even though we couldn't really afford this option given my new work arrangement.

Luckily, Vince did not give up. He really did have a vision. So the more we talked about it and the more time I spent with Zachary, the more I grew to understand what a house in the country could mean for us. And that's how we ended up settling somewhere in the middle – buying a house in a small town (civilization for me) in the country (cow pastures for Vince).

You can never know for sure if you've chosen the right route until you've tried it.

The reality is that you can never know for sure if you've chosen the right route until you've tried it. But you have to start somewhere. The advice I always hear from women who have made the transition to flexible work is to take a step, even if it's a small step. At least you'll be further ahead than where you started. Chances are you will learn something about yourself, too – like I did. I learned that the sky didn't come crashing down just because I moved to the country. In fact, a brighter blue sky opened up, offering me many uninterrupted hours to enjoy Zachary and his growing zest for life.

To translate your vision into real life, you need to figure out what kind of flexible work arrangement makes sense, given your motherhood goals, your career ambitions and your financial situation. There will always be good arguments as to why your job won't suit a flexible work arrangement or why it's crazy to start your own business. Ignore them all. I have seen women turn just about every kind of job or skill into flexible work arrangements for themselves. You can do it, too.

What's your Flex Appeal Profile?

Trying to decide what kind of work arrangement will work for you can be stressful, but it doesn't have to be. There are pros and cons for each type of work arrangement – whether it's teleworking, working for yourself or working part time. But what's really crucial is for you to pinpoint which aspects of your work will be most important to you when you move to a more flexible work arrangement. Based on many discussions with women who have made the transition to flexible work, answering these four key questions will help you determine your priorities when it comes to balancing work and your children:

- How much flexibility can you live with?
- How important is career advancement to you?
- How much risk can you handle?
- What does money really mean to you?

I like to think of these as the four facets that make up a woman's Flex Appeal Profile. Determining your own Flex Appeal Profile will help you evaluate the various work options available to you, and decide whether or not they fit with your "new" priorities. You may think that you're already clear about what kind of work arrangement you want. Great! Just make sure that the work option you're considering is based on your new objectives, not what was important to you before you decided you needed more time with your children.

Let me give you some examples of what I'm talking about. While promotions and raises may have been the trophies you used to covet, your new motivations may be to have less responsibility and work fewer hours so you can spend time with your new baby. Or you may decide that while you want a flexible work arrangement, you're simply not willing or can't afford to give up more than 20 percent of your salary. Or perhaps you now find yourself willing to risk going out on your own to gain more control over your time, when you used to think job security was everything.

The only way to build your Flex Appeal Profile is to work through these four questions and be honest with yourself about how you really feel. Only then will you be able to determine the right option for you.

How much flexibility can you live with?

If you think back to the last chapter in which you were designing your vision, you answered questions about what hours you would ideally like to work and what kind of flexibility might suit your job. Flexibility works both ways, so the more flexibility you think you want, the more you should be prepared to give back to your employer or to your customers.

If you think you want a lot of flexibility in your new work arrangement, then some of your options might include running your own business or negotiating a part-time flexible work schedule where you can set some or all of your own hours each week. This is the kind of flexibility that could make it possible for you to be your baby's primary caregiver, or take off in the middle of the day to attend your child's nursery school graduation. The flip side of having a lot of flexibility to spend time with your kids is that you will most likely end up having to finish an assignment at 10:00 p.m., or working five days straight to get a project done. You may also have to consider finding an emergency caregiver to help you through a busy period. So if flexibility is the most important thing to you, ask yourself whether you can live with an ever-changing schedule, both in terms of your time with your kids and your work schedule.

For Judy the answer was yes. A 39-year-old mother of two children, ages four and six, Judy gave up her job as a travel agent to run her own specialty gift basket company out of her home. After the birth of her first child, she found it increasingly difficult to liaise with her travel clients over the phone while being the primary caregiver. She wanted more flexibility over the hours she worked. So she started a small gift basket business and made

Is working from home right for you?

Benefits – you get to:

- set your own hours (or at least some of them)
- work in your sweats and throw in a load of laundry during work hours
- save money on gas, work clothes and lunches
- attend your child's field trip or volunteer in the classroom
- be at home when your child is sick

Challenges – you may have to:

- be very self-disciplined (no one will be watching over you)
- give up living space in your house to create a home office
- get out during the day to fight the isolation
- work hard to ensure you are still visible at work with your boss and coworkers
- learn to turn work off when you're with your family

Is working flexible hours for you?

Benefits – you get to:

- work more independently
- set some or all of your hours
- schedule time with your child without any hassle
- avoid office politics and time-wasting meetings

Challenges – you may have to:

- learn to live with collisions between your work time and time with your kids
- work extra hard to show you are just as committed to your job as before
- take sole responsibility for getting your work done
- find affordable flexible child care (which can be difficult to find)

---

specialty chocolates and candies out of her home. Judy was willing to accept the unpredictability of not always knowing how much money she would bring in, or of getting an emergency order that would keep her working three days straight (night and day). In return, she got the flexibility of being available to her children when they needed her.

Maybe you're envisioning a work arrangement that's more predictable and less flexible. Perhaps you would prefer to know exactly what hours you'll work each week and what kind of workload you'll be responsible for. You might consider a three- or four-day workweek, or working the same five half-days each week. Many women prefer firm boundaries for when work starts and stops, leaving less chance that work will flow into their time off. Having set hours makes it easier to plan meetings and face-to-face interactions with colleagues and your supervisor. Lining up day care is easier when you know your hours are fixed, and it also helps if you want to plan things with your children.

Thirty-year-old Sophie wanted the predictability of going into an office and job she was familiar with the same three days every week. Sophie knew she wanted to work part time or not at all after she had her first child, Ashley. As a financial services communications manager, she was able to secure a three-day-a-week contract to work Monday through Wednesday each week. Sophie liked knowing that every week she could get out of the house from 8:30 a.m. to 5:30 p.m. to interact with adults, work on interesting projects and have some personal time at lunch to run errands. She also needed a predictable schedule because of her child-care arrangement. Her mother-in-law agreed to close down her beauty salon business one day a week to care for Ashley, but it had to be the same day every week.

You may find yourself relating to Judy or Sophie, or you may be looking for a flexible work arrangement that falls somewhere between the two. Ask yourself: How much flexibility do I really need to achieve my vision? A good rule of thumb is the more predictable you want your work schedule to be, the less flexible your work arrangement needs to be, and vice versa.

Nancy's Flex Appeal Profile

Flexibility was her number one priority

- wanted lots of flexibility, including reduced hours
- accepted risk that she could lose her part-time status at any time
- understood she would have to revise her career aspirations
- was willing to trade off income, but not more than 40 percent

When Nancy adopted her son, now 11, she didn't want to miss any part of his life. She and her husband had waited a long time to have a child and she was pretty sure that he was going to be her only one. As a reporter for a major newspaper, she also knew that staying home full time wouldn't be good for her or her son. Part-time flexible hours seemed like the perfect balance. When she approached her employer, he agreed to let her try it out for six months. Twelve years later, Nancy still works part time for the same newspaper, because she loves the flexibility it gives her.

"I have worked for a number of editors and on various beats over the years, and I have still managed to stay in a part-time role," says Nancy. She attributes her success to her willingness to be flexible when her job requires it. Though she is scheduled to put in three days a week, she has no problem putting in four when she is working on a particular story or a tight deadline. In fact, when she's been really interested in a story she has been known to work five days over a two- to three-week period to get the assignment done. She also does interviews from home on her days off if that's the only day that she can schedule the call. Nancy is quick to point out, however, that you have to balance the need to bend with the need to be firm. Knowing when you've reached your limit and learning to say no are important, too.

Working a flexible schedule meant that Nancy needed flexible child care – and that she had to pay for it. When her son was an infant, she ended up paying for full-time care just to get an in-home caregiver who could cover all the hours she needed to work. By the time her son was three, she was fortunate to find a progressive day-care facility willing to take him part time. Now that he's a full-time student, he goes to a friend's house after school on the days that Nancy can't be home with him.

Since taking the plunge into flexible work, Nancy has adjusted her aspirations for herself. "When I was young, I thought I wanted eventually to become a section editor," she says. "That dream has never come back, but I don't feel like I've given up because I get a lot of satisfaction from my writing. With writing I am challenged to give my personal best every day and this is my reward."

Like many women who have shifted to more flexible work, Nancy has surprised herself at her desire to continue to work part time even though her son is in his early teens. "I used to say that when my son was in school full time I would go back to work full time," says Nancy. "But he still needs me. Life gets more complicated as kids get older. My son gets lots of homework and he needs my help getting organized. Plus I need to find time to squeeze in extracurricular activities, such as skating lessons and baseball games. And then there's our weekly ritual where he and a friend come home for lunch. I wouldn't miss it for anything."

How important is career advancement to you?

Now there's an interesting question. Most women I spoke with were very clear that they had given up career opportunities – chances for promotions and raises, or chances to grow their own businesses – in order to gain more time with their children. Given their new priorities, some even felt happy that they had less responsibility or less pressure to climb a career ladder. Yet many of these women still struggled with what seemed to them an unfair trade-off – losing out on opportunities that they would have had if they'd stayed in the workforce full time.

There is simply no quick fix for this dilemma of consciously slowing down to be with your kids, but not wanting to slow down your career advancement. Almost all women switching to flexible work arrangements face it and chances are you will, too. Working more flexible hours – and in particular less hours overall – almost always involves trading off career or business growth. Think about it. How often do you read about a successful woman entrepreneur or senior manager who is working part time? Now that's not to say that you shouldn't continue to strive toward achieving career or business goals you set for yourself, you just may have to adjust them to suit the reality of your new situation.

If you know you want to reduce the level of responsibility that you currently handle, then be prepared to live with trade-offs, such as having a job with less status or losing out on interesting assignments because you're not in the office as much as your colleagues. Betty, an analyst for an insurance company, agreed to take on a different position in order to go back to work part time after having her first child. Mother of 21-month-old Janet (with another baby on the way), Betty took on more systems-related work that would suit her new part-time hours. While Betty does not consider her work a "career," she does feel good about the contributions she is making to both her employer and to the family income. Best of all, she enjoys being an integral part of her child's life. "Working part time allows me to stay connected to my daughter and watch her day-to-day development," says Betty. "She could learn three new words this week and I know I'll be around to hear at least two of them."

Should you decide, however, that you're not willing to sacrifice career growth and advancement for a more flexible

Is a compressed workweek for you?

Benefits – you get to:

- maintain the same income and job status
- work the same number of hours as before, making it easier for your supervisor and coworkers to accept your new arrangement
- enjoy an extra day off each week

Challenges – you may have to:

- adjust to longer, more tiring work days
- find caregivers willing to cover off ten-hour days
- learn to manage your boss's high expectations of you (it is likely his or her expectations won't change, even though your schedule will)

---

work arrangement, then your options may be more limited. In other words, you may want to consider *not* cutting back on your hours, or at least not cutting them back substantially. A condensed workweek or teleworking might give you more flexibility with your time without actually reducing your hours. If you're committed to shifting to part-time work anyway, be realistic about what this will mean for you. One study of women managers who had shifted to part-time work showed that many of these women had been successful at working fewer hours and still being promoted. Not surprisingly though, the study, conducted by McGill and Purdue Universities and called "Improvising New Careers," also revealed that they worked awfully hard to do it. Reduced hours for them often meant going from a 50- to 60-hour week to a 30- to 40-hour week – not exactly the kind of part-time hours you probably have in mind!

Most women who shift to flexible work arrangements are taking one foot off the career track. The question is, how far off are you willing to step to get what you want?

Susan's Flex Appeal Profile

Taking a step down the career ladder brought peace of mind

- wanted a fixed three-day workweek, close to home
- wanted less responsibility at work so she could focus more energy on her children
- accepted the risk of slowing down her career
- worked out a base salary that she could accept

Susan learned the hard way that she needed to be more assertive about the work/family balance in her life. Mother of Ben, seven, and Katie, five, Susan went back to work full time after each of her children was born. She was burning herself out working six days a week as the executive director of a charity and was beginning to feel that life was too short. She wanted more time to enjoy her children while they were still young.

Susan's job was technically a four-day-a-week position, but she was working a minimum of five days along with many weeknights and weekends, to keep up with her senior management duties. Even when she wasn't at work, Susan found the stress of work bubbling over into her family and social life. "I remember being out with friends and sitting there feeling bored," says Susan. "That's when it struck me that I couldn't relax enough to enjoy myself." Susan became concerned about her health, and the last straw came when she and her husband decided they were not going to have any more children. "My husband had the vasectomy, and I thought, these are the only two kids I'm ever going to have," she says. "If I don't get out soon, I won't fully enjoy them."

Susan knew that she needed a job with fewer hours and less responsibility. She was tired of being the one in charge of solving every problem that arose at her organization. She wasn't, however, willing to start at the bottom again. She agreed to play a more minor managerial role, though she still wanted a job that suited her skills and senior-level experience. Susan spent an entire year looking for the perfect fit. Because she had really thought through what she wanted, she knew when she hit upon the right opportunity. She eventually took a three-day-a-week job as an allocations manager at another charity, where she helps dole out funds to not-for-profit organizations.

Susan's new job has given her exactly what she wanted – her family life back. Where she used to rush out in the mornings, yelling at her kids to hurry up, she now walks her son to school and actually gets to chat with some of the neighbors. She is more involved with Katie's school and can take Ben to after-school activities like Beavers and soccer practice. On one of the afternoons Katie is at school, Susan catches up on household chores so that she can spend weekends freely with her family.

Susan speaks frankly about the challenges of downsizing her job and her career. "It was an emotional shift for me, taking a step down," she says. "I had to adjust to the fact that I am no longer an 'executive director' and that, in subtle ways, I no longer have the final say on things." But having made the shift to flexible work, Susan insists she will never go back to the kind of demanding job she had before. "I went into this thinking, there's got to be a better way to live," she says. "I've learned that there is."

How much risk can you handle?

Today's workplace is ready for women to think of themselves as their own bosses and seek the flexible work arrangements they want. While this can be very exciting, it can also feel like the biggest risk of your life.

Ask yourself: How much risk can I actually live with in exchange for a more flexible work arrangement? Most people would see having their own business as the riskiest option of all, believing that it is difficult to depend on a secure monthly income when you're working for yourself. But money is not the only risk factor. What about the risk of not getting along

Is job sharing right for you?

Benefits – you get to:

- keep the job intact (managers like this element)
- stay in the loop because you've got an office partner to keep you informed
- call on your partner when emergencies arise and you need someone to fill in
- take advantage of bouncing ideas off a coworker

Challenges – you may have to:

- find a new partner if your current job-share partner changes her mind
- communicate with your partner daily
- give up half your salary
- spend less time socializing with colleagues
- deal with some frustrated coworkers and clients who don't like having to work with two people

with your job-sharing partner, or the risk of having the nature of your job changed because you won't be available five days a week?

Monika, a 31-year-old single mother, believes that working for others is more risky than working for herself. Once a controller for a $4-million company, Monika grew tired of the long hours and immense pressure that left her with little time to spend with her two daughters, now eight and 11. Today she provides accounting and bookkeeping services to small- and medium-sized businesses. Monika says that leaving the corporate sector was like jumping off a cliff, yet she's grateful she made that jump. She found starting her own business to be an incredibly liberating experience. She believes that by working for herself she is much more in control of who she works with, when she gets paid and her overall success.

Is running your own business for you?

Benefits – you get to:

- have more control over your time
- choose your coworkers or employees
- potentially enjoy more tax breaks
- avoid office politics

Challenges – you may have to:

- deal with uncertainty about how much money you'll make each month
- oversee every aspect of the business (marketing, bookkeeping, etc.)
- be prepared to motivate yourself
- arrange and pay for your own benefits

Other risks to think about include not being able to say no to extra work or coming in for meetings on your days off, not getting recognized for your hard work or being left out of the loop when you are working from home. There's also a risk that your coworkers will resent your "special treatment" – especially if you are the only person in your office or department working flexible hours.

What kinds of risk are you prepared to take to make your schedule work? Think about this before you make any firm decisions.

Joanne's Flex Appeal Profile

Taking risks has really paid off

- wanted maximum flexibility to adjust to her daughter's changing schedule
- made a conscious decision to slow the growth of her business
- was prepared to take risks every day to maintain work/family balance
- accepted major financial sacrifices to achieve her vision

Joanne, an author and entrepreneur, is a risk-taker. Seven years ago, she started her own business specializing in educating companies about women and money. Joanne had begun to build a blue-chip client roster and had her own national television program when she learned she was pregnant. Weeks before her daughter, Kate, was born, Joanne closed a deal to train employees of a major financial institution. But the trainer she had hired to actually do the work bailed out on her. Joanne took a big business risk by asking the client to put off the training for six to nine months until she returned from maternity leave. He agreed.

When Joanne returned to work she felt profound guilt when she was away from Kate, missing out on her daughter's development. So she shifted to a three-day workweek, which gave her two more days with her daughter. This shift required what Joanne calls huge financial concessions: "I gave up the TV show and essentially I put off growing my business as quickly as I had originally planned."

Acknowledging that limiting the growth of her business is tough, Joanne is adamant that she would not take on a new business opportunity if it would require changing her schedule. She is grateful to her two devoted employees for their support and their willingness to work around her daughter's ever-changing schedule.

Joanne is happy with the new balance she's created. She doesn't take life as seriously as she used to. "One minute I'm on the floor wrapped in dress-up scarves and surrounded by stuffed animals, and a couple of hours later I'm downtown presenting to a group of executives at a large accounting firm," she says. "The carryover of being fun and carefree during my morning with Kate is very powerful."

Although Joanne is perceived as highly successful by many businessmen and women, she admits to continually worrying about her business failing. She pressures herself to bring in a certain amount of income. She has to work at not being too hard on herself and at accepting there is only so much she can do, given her schedule. "At the end of the day I ask myself: Did I do my best today?" says Joanne. "Whether I gave it 30 percent or 100 percent, then that was my best effort that day."

What does money really mean to you?

Money is an important factor in decisions women make about flexible work. While this comes as no revelation, it does come with a warning: Money can lure women away from their vision very quickly. Money is not just about having a roof overhead and paying the bills. Money can equal power in the relationship between spouses. For many women, the more they contribute to the household income the more equal they feel with their husband. Money also makes women feel like contributing members of society because they are paid for what they do. For many it is recognition for a job well done. Income can also be a significant part of how women measure their own self-worth – even though most women are loath to admit it.

Is a part-time or reduced workweek right for you?

Benefits – you get to:

- work fewer hours and have more time with your kids
- choose what days or hours you work (although not always)
- involve yourself less in office politics
- enjoy a less hectic work schedule with a lesser likelihood of burnout

Challenges – you may have to:

- accept that your lack of visibility in the office could affect future work opportunities
- spend less time socializing with colleagues
- take a cut in your salary
- accommodate a change to your workload and level of responsibility

All of these issues come into play when you decide what kind of flexible work arrangement is right for you. You may start off with a vision of working three days a week, but when you think about making only 60 percent of your salary, you may decide four days will suit you better. Some women who switch to part-time work become uncomfortable when they realize that their spouse's work suddenly comes first, because his job earns the major income.

Be conscious of how much money you really need and want, and why. There is no right or wrong answer. You're not a bad mother if you choose to work four days instead of three because you don't want to sell your house or have your job come second to your spouse's. Your vision is about what you are comfortable with – not what anyone else thinks is the right thing to do.

Jackie's Flex Appeal Profile

The job was more important than the money

- was determined to do her old full-time job on a new part-time basis
- was not worried that working fewer hours would limit her career growth
- believed the only risk she faced was not spending enough time with her daughter
- ranked money as less of a priority than doing a job she loved

Jackie loves her job. As a support worker for parents with young children suffering from HIV/AIDS, she helps more than 150 families each year. But after having her first child, Jackie began to doubt whether she would be able to return to work and leave her baby, Rachel, with another caregiver. To ease back into her job, Jackie negotiated to work a temporary part-time contract out of her home to give her three months to adjust and to find child care for her daughter. The contract helped to remind Jackie how important her work was to her and those three months helped her realize that working at home wasn't an option. She needed to be out of the house to be productive.

Today Jackie spends anywhere from two and a half to three and a half days a week working at her organization's office. She admits she often puts in up to another full day at home to keep up with the demands of her job. Because of the odd hours she works (some nights and early mornings), Jackie needs the flexibility of an in-home caregiver for her daughter, even though the cost seemed prohibitive initially. "I'm basically losing money by working," says Jackie. "I know a lot of people would think I'm crazy, but I really do love what I do and I find it incredibly rewarding. The adult stimulation is invaluable. I feel useful outside the home and I feel like I'm not putting my career on hold completely. I also think I'm a better parent at home because I work."

Jackie acknowledges that there are many challenges associated with trying to juggle a part-time workload and part-time care of Rachel. "I feel like I'm never really one place or the other," says Jackie. "When I'm at work I'm often thinking about what Rachel's doing and when I'm at home I find myself thinking about work. I never really get rid of this inner conflict, but I have found ways of minimizing it. I just remind myself that I have the two things I want most – a fulfilling job and an opportunity to be at home with my daughter."

It pays to be creative

Whenever I hear women's stories about work and family, I am struck by their focus on "what can be" rather than "what is." Women who are successful at securing the right kind of flexible work arrangements for themselves are very creative. They look for work options to suit their vision, and if they can't find a job that fits, they often create one.

Don't let yourself be intimidated if no one in your department or your company is working flexible or part-time hours. Disregard the naysayers who warn you about the difficulties of running your own business or downshifting your career. Remember your vision. Hold on to your passion and the reason you're contemplating this change (think back to one of those recent "mommy moments"). Then move to the next chapter and build your plan of attack.

CHAPTER 4

Don't Wing It, Have a Plan!

"When I decided to start my own practice, my business partner and I spent a lot of time discussing the philosophy of the practice we wanted to run. We both wanted more control over our lives and more flexibility to spend time with our children. After much deliberation, the plan evolved to include three doctors each working three and a half days a week. While the medical community didn't take us seriously right away, we were instantly busy with patients and have built a successful practice. And the result is that I'm baking cinnamon buns as we speak and picking up my kids after soccer practice today."

Lanice, the mother of Willis, 13, Eric, ten, and Minetta, eight, has been running her own medical practice for eight years.

I have to be honest. Aside from arranging child care for Zachary three days a week and knowing I would have a lot less money to spend, I did not really have a plan for managing my own reduced workweek. I didn't have to sell it to an employer or convince coworkers. And I wasn't about to call up my clients and ask their permission to take Mondays and Fridays off. So

Vince and I basically just winged it. Luckily for us, after six initial months of smoothing out the bumps, it has worked out.

I do not recommend that you take my approach, unless you welcome the excruciating stress headaches that go with it. It is better to come up with a good plan for several reasons. It can help you anticipate and work through some potential issues that may crop up in your new work arrangement, such as convincing clients that their work will get done even if you're not in on Fridays. Thinking through all the nitty-gritty details will give you a more realistic picture of how your new vision will unfold. A plan also forces you to think about setting firm boundaries up front. That way you can avoid your boss calling you on your days off or a client showing up at your door while you're bathing your children (don't laugh; it happened to a woman I know).

Thoughtful planning will also help you put something in writing that you can share with your spouse, a prospective business partner or the boss you're trying to convince. It will give your negotiations with your boss an undeniable advantage because you'll be clearer about what you're trying to sell and why it will benefit the company.

Do your homework

In my experience as a consultant, I have learned over and over again the value of doing my homework (it's funny that I didn't learn this at school). Before I meet with a client, I take the time to really think about what I hope to get out of our discussion. If it's a new client, I do research on their organization in advance of the meeting. That way I am most likely to get the consulting contract I'm after and achieve my goals.

Preparing to make a major life change requires the same strategic approach. If you plan to propose a flexible work arrangement to your boss, the best place to start is in your company's human resources department, if you have one. Seek out examples of other women who work flexible hours in your company. They will probably be able to offer you some great pointers on how to negotiate your flex work proposal, and what you should expect if you go flex. And you can refer to them as examples of flex arrangements that are working within your company – assuming they are working – when you pitch your boss on your new flexible schedule.

Another way to convince your employer of the pluses of a more flexible work arrangement is to gather studies and articles that show the many advantages to being a flex-friendly company. Basically, you need to show your boss that flexible hours not only work for the employee, but they have benefits for the company, too.

For support material to include in your proposal, try these websites:

- www.workfamily.com
- www.catalystwomen.org
- www.familiesandwork.org

It's also helpful and reassuring to discuss your plans with other women in your community who have made the transition to flexible work. You might find them at your local park or at a drop-in program for moms with young children. Or try putting a notice up at your local grocery store or in your local paper and say that you're looking to speak with moms who work part-time or flex hours.

I was fortunate that a member of the Welcome Wagon (a Canada-wide organization that welcomes newcomers to the neighborhood) came to my door just weeks after we had moved into our new house. The woman who visited me (she was a dead ringer for June Cleaver) asked if she could help me with anything. I told her I needed help finding child care for my son. She directed me to a mother down the street who had just gone through the process of finding child care for her two boys. This other mother led me to my current caregiver, and also turned out to be a great support in other ways. She, too, was a business owner who worked three days a week.

How to find women to talk to about flexible work:

- ask friends or family members if they know mothers who work part time
- seek out women at a local park or drop-in program for children
- start a support group and advertise it
- contact community organizations such as churches, service clubs or libraries
- ask your human resources department or other employees for names
- in Canada, contact your local Welcome Wagon (www.welcomewagon.ca)

If you're serious about starting your own business, then you should try to connect with other women entrepreneurs who can help prepare you for the road ahead. You do not want to talk to entrepreneurs who are running multimillion-dollar companies. After all, how many women have you read about who have built a multimillion-dollar company working on a part-time basis? You do want to speak with other women whose primary objective in running their own business is to have more flexibility for their children. Hearing other women's stories may help alleviate some of the fears you're probably experiencing about going out on your own.

There are also plenty of resources for women who are looking to network, write a business plan or simply learn about the basics of self-employment.

Helpful websites for women entrepreneurs:

- www.royalbank.com/sme
- www.bwni.com
- www.onlinewbc.gov

Start with a soft sell

If you feel anxious about making changes to your life, it's safe to assume that your boss will feel some anxiety about changing the way you work, too. So instead of marching into his office one day and demanding that he let you work part time, why not let him get used to the idea first? Depending on the relationship you have with your boss, you may be able to informally drop the news that you are considering switching to a more flexible work arrangement. At the end of an update meeting, you could mention that you have been investigating the benefits of working more flexible hours. Or you could ask your boss to grab a sandwich or coffee with you in order to talk about your workload, then introduce the idea. Follow up your conversation with any research you've found that extols the virtues of flexible work arrangements. Your boss can review it at his leisure.

If you're pregnant or on maternity leave, this may be a good time to start talking to your boss about switching to a flexible work arrangement. This may help alleviate his anxiety about you not coming back at all and make him more receptive to your request. If you're at all concerned that telling him early may jeopardize your chances of returning to your job, wait until a few weeks before you're expected back at work to suggest a change.

The same soft sell is a good idea if you are contemplating starting your own business. You have an opportunity to begin connecting with prospective clients, informally, before you're actually trying to sell them anything. Let them know that you're in the early stages of developing your business idea and ask how they might use your services, what they would be looking for and what kind of budget they might have to spend. Search out other individuals or small firms in the same industry that could also lend you some valuable knowledge or advice. Just make sure you position yourself as a noncompetitor who would really appreciate hearing about their extensive experience in the field (few people will refuse an opportunity to blow their own horn).

Build a team of supporters

Before you officially pitch your boss on a flexible work arrangement, go to coworkers or clients whom you feel comfortable talking to about your plans. Ask them to suggest how you could make your new arrangement work for them. These people will be affected by your new work arrangement; approaching them before you make the change will show them that you care about the impact it will have on them and encourage their buy-in. Then you can go to your boss with a proposal that offers practical suggestions for ensuring that clients get the help they need and for staying connected to your coworkers. Or, even better, you might think of a coworker or client who really likes you and may be willing to support your request in writing or by speaking with your boss. If you're at all uncomfortable approaching anyone prior to speaking with your boss about a flexible work arrangement, then don't. Not everyone works in an environment where this makes sense.

Building a team of supporters can be equally as important in running a successful business. Being the boss often requires expertise that you may not have, such as marketing, bookkeeping or staff management. Why not build a small team of advisers or supporters who can bring some of these skills to your business? Some people may be willing to be advisers free of charge if they see an opportunity to network with other businesspeople or trade skills with you (for example, you might provide them with marketing support, while they provide you with accounting and legal advice). Many small businesses today have gone this route. Do you have a friend or family member who has the kind of expertise you need? How about a past colleague or someone who already runs a successful business in your community?

Get serious, start writing

Now it's time to put your plan in writing. A written proposal is important whether it's for a start-up business or a new work arrangement at your old job.

Before you start your own business, you need to develop your business model, including what you're selling, what your work arrangement will be, how you're going to be profitable and so on. Think of it like writing a proposal to yourself. It forces you to commit to your vision and think concretely about how it will work.

If you're trying to sell your employer on a new work arrangement, then a written plan tells him that you're very serious. Remember Eliza, the computer programmer who went in to tell her boss she was quitting to have more time with her two daughters? She was sure that her boss would not even consider a more flexible work arrangement – so sure that she was willing to give up her job. When her boss saw she was serious about leaving, he agreed to give her everything she wanted. I'm not advocating that you threaten to quit if you don't get what you want – unless, of course, you feel so strongly about it that you're prepared for your employer to send you packing.

Besides showing that you're serious, a written proposal makes you organize your thoughts.

Besides showing that you're serious, a written proposal forces you to organize your thoughts. "Having a written plan makes you think things through," says Pat Brown from First Tennessee Bank. "I really like it when employees lay out the pros and cons of the flexible work arrangement they're proposing. You do need to be clear about how all the work will be covered under your new arrangement. In other words, you have to think about it from the perspective of your manager."

The most significant benefit in writing a proposal is that it forces you to come up with good answers to the tough questions your boss is likely to raise. This will make it much more difficult for your boss to say no without at least giving your proposal some thoughtful consideration.

Create a winning proposal

A well-written proposal should be clear, concise and easy to read, with sections clearly identified using subheads. It can be anywhere from two to 20 pages (I'd suggest no more than ten) in length, depending on how much detail will convince your supervisor to say yes. Ideally, the proposal should convey your idea so clearly that anyone reading it for the first time will get the gist of it without further explanation. While you'll want to discuss the key points of the proposal with your boss in person, keep in mind that she will likely want to review it thoroughly on her own and possibly pass it on to other people in the company.

Always consider who will be reading the proposal. If it's your boss, think about what kind of language excites her and what format she responds to best. Will she prefer an outline or a full-blown detailed plan? Does she like to receive documents well ahead of scheduled meetings so that she can review them carefully, or does she prefer to have proposals presented to her? Have you anticipated her key concerns and addressed them in your proposal?

The same principles apply if you're writing the proposal as a rough business outline – and I do stress "rough." Following the proposal writing suggestions in this chapter is a good start. A proposal is something you can share with a potential partner or your spouse; you can even refer back to it as a roadmap to keep you on the right track. It should therefore be organized to paint a clear picture of what you're trying to accomplish. For others who are launching a more sophisticated business model, you will need a formal business plan to help you deal with complex issues such as incorporation of your company, bank financing or taxes. For help writing a business plan, you can check out the websites for women entrepreneurs included in this chapter (page 63) or purchase one of many software programs (for around $100) that offer a business plan template for you to fill in.

This part of the book will show you what a great proposal should look like and help you identify and think through all the important details of your new flexible work arrangement. Once you're ready to sit down and start writing your proposal, you can refer to the more detailed proposal writing exercise at the back of the book (page 155).

Start with a convincing introduction

The first page should introduce your plan with snappy and convincing language. Give your boss a feel for what you're proposing, while selling him on the concept at the same time. Make sure you focus on the benefits to him and the company, such as reassigning some of your work to someone with a lesser salary or attracting you to stay with the company for the long-term. If you can tie what you're trying to do to a company policy or mission statement, by all means do it. You should also be clear about why you're proposing this new arrangement. Try to present a balance between wanting more time with your child and wanting to continue your work as a valuable, dedicated employee. You may also want to throw in some favorable statistics or other supportive information you've found regarding flex hours at other companies (refer to the websites that offer good support materials on page 61).

Sue, a public health nurse, knew before she had her first baby that she would want to return to work part time. So, before she even went on maternity leave, she started thinking about what might work in her department. She came up with the perfect job-sharing partner and plan. Then she spent three months trying to convince her boss to agree to it. She eventually figured out that her boss was resisting because she thought a job-sharing arrangement would be more complicated – that it would take more time to manage two people in the same role. In response, Sue developed a written proposal showing that job sharing would actually be less work for her boss because she wouldn't have to hire a new full-time person for Sue's job. By hiring Sue and her partner, Sue's boss would save months of poring over résumés and conducting interviews. She would also avoid the investment of time it would take to bring the new person up to speed. Her boss finally agreed and Sue got her part-time, job-sharing arrangement.

If your proposal is actually your business plan, write the executive summary like you're pitching an investor (whether you're the main investor or the bank is). This summary is a brief description of your business model, why you think it will work and what kind of objectives you've set for yourself. Your objectives should be measurable and realistic; for example, you plan to have 15 regular customers by the end of six months, or you want to be earning $30,000 at the end of one year.

Outline your proposed work arrangement

When you are outlining your proposal, you should be clear about the schedule you plan to work, where you plan to work and how your job responsibilities will be redefined. Or in the case of your own business, you should outline what your new job responsibilities will be.

Start with a description of the days and hours you want to work, and how this new schedule makes sense for your key responsibilities. For instance, if a big part of your job involves teamwork, make sure you show how your new schedule will still allow you to meet with team members on a regular basis.

Or show a new schedule that ensures you will attend departmental meetings every Tuesday morning. If you'll be working for yourself, describe how your new schedule will fit with the demands of your children, the business and your customers.

Next, describe your proposed workplace. If you're planning to work from a home office for part or all of your hours, talk about the set-up you envision. How will you ensure you will be connected to the office from your home? What kind of technology will be in place: e-mail, fax, separate phone line, cell phone or pager? How will coworkers or clients reach you when you're not in the office? What kind of child-care arrangement will you have in place, so that you are free from distractions? These are all important questions whether you plan to work for yourself or for someone else.

The more specific you are about how you see the structure of your new job and how you plan to reassign certain responsibilities, the less your boss will have to think about. To be very specific, you really need to understand how much time you spend on different aspects of your job. You may find it helpful to mentally walk through a typical week at work, writing down how long it takes you to do certain tasks. Ask yourself whether there are ways of eliminating some of those tasks or at least reassigning them. For instance, you may spend 20 percent of your time in meetings. Do you need to attend every meeting in order to do your job? Or you may find that you spend 10 percent of your time sending follow-up faxes. Could an administrative assistant handle that instead? Employers love it when you come up with a way to save them money, so if you can envision reassigning part of your work to someone at a lower salary level, this will make your proposal much more appealing.

Thirty-five-year-old Patricia was successful at convincing her employer, a magazine publishing company, to let her work a reduced workweek after the birth of her daughter, Ava, now one. She presented her boss with a proposal that clearly laid out how 20 percent of her responsibilities could be reassigned to an assistant from her department. As a result, her job as a sales promotion manager was reduced from five to four days a week. Here's how she suggested her new job be structured:

Job responsibilities she kept:

- creating and executing promotions
- performing client presentations
- developing sales promotion materials
- negotiating event sponsorships
- planning and creating advertising and publicity campaigns
- managing budgets

Job responsibilities delegated to an assistant:

- obtaining client approvals
- managing contest details
- distributing free magazines to clients
- writing an on-line newsletter
- executing the publicity campaigns

If you are planning to run your own business, you need to understand how your work will unfold, given your business objectives and your new flexible schedule. Is it realistic to think that you can make the income you are projecting within the framework of the three-day workweek you're proposing? Have you taken into account the time you will have to spend on business-related responsibilities like invoicing or marketing? Projecting your new work plan into concrete hours and duties will help you determine whether you need to readjust some of your business objectives.

Show how you will remain accessible

Appearing accessible and being available 24 hours a day are two very different things. I learned this very quickly when I moved out of the city, away from most of my clients. Many questioned whether I would be as available to attend meetings or deal with issues as quickly as before, given my new country location. But because of the way I manage my schedule and my clients, this has never been an issue in the three years since I moved.

Your boss will want to know that you are accessible when unforeseen situations arise: an emergency (they can't find a file), a client crisis (there's a period missing in an annual report), or a last-minute departmental meeting (to discuss why your group has been using 50 percent more office supplies than it did last year). Seriously, though, you need to outline how you will stay connected to work, without being a slave to your cell phone every time you take your children to the park.

If you are reducing your work hours, you *should not* offer to be accessible all the time. What you should offer are suggestions for keeping in touch with your boss, coworkers and clients as much as is required for your job.

I have figured out a way to keep clients from calling on my days off or getting frustrated if I don't return their calls right away. To begin with, if I'm working on a fairly intense project with a client (lots of communicating back and forth), I call them the day before I'm off just to check in and remind them that I won't be in the office the next day. That way they're forewarned. It also gives them an opportunity to speak with me if they need to. Then I leave very clear instructions on my voice mail that I will not be checking my messages on my day off, especially when I know I'll be out at the zoo or at a class with Zachary.

Asking your employer to change your work arrangement is like applying for a new job.

Think about your job responsibilities or your customer's needs and then imagine ways to ensure you can meet those responsibilities when you won't be in the office five days a week. You may decide that checking in on a day off makes sense when you're working on an intense project or have a tight deadline. Or you might want to commit to attending a monthly departmental or client meeting even when it falls on a day you don't normally work. Be flexible and creative, and I guarantee your boss and your customers will appreciate it.

Explain how you're going to make it work

In many ways, asking your employer to change your work arrangement is like applying for a new job. You have to sell yourself for the role you're creating. This is your opportunity to outline the key skills and expertise that you think are needed for this job – both the actual work and the flexible arrangement part – and explain why you fit the bill. You should emphasize past accomplishments to illustrate your track record in certain areas. For instance, if you're proposing to work out of your home, you may want to show how you have been successful at working independently in the past. If you're asking for more flexible hours that will require some juggling and discipline, you should highlight past examples of your ability to manage several different projects at once and get the job done.

It is also important to talk about how you will manage any roadblocks that arise due to your new flexible work arrangement, according to Wendy Hirschberg, associate director of the Office for Retention at Ernst & Young and a flexible worker herself. "You need to show your employer how you will continue to work closely with team members, how you'll meet deadlines and, most importantly, how you'll resolve conflicts that arise," she says. "This is all part of managing up, which is basically helping your boss understand how it will work."

Starting your own business also requires a very different way of managing your workload, especially if you're planning to do something you've never done before. What are the key skills you have that will be critical to your success? Where will you need to bring in outside expertise? Think through what your new business needs to be successful, such as accounting software, a local print shop or a marketing adviser. This will help ensure you put the critical resources in place before you actually launch the business, and that you have realistic goals for the number of hours you want to work.

Paint your new financial picture

Unless you plan to work a compressed workweek, your income and benefits are likely to change. If you're pitching a new work arrangement to your employer, I would try to position it as a cost savings to your company. Make sure you include the salary you expect to make and don't forget to factor in the extra time you will have to put in to stay connected on your days off (and believe me, you will put in extra time). Instead of reducing your salary to 60 percent for three days of work, suggest 65 percent.

Also be clear about the benefits you hope to receive. Your employer's cost to include you in the company's benefit plan will likely not change just because you're shifting to a more flexible work arrangement, but you still may have to convince him to keep you on the company plan. If you are proposing to work less than 20 hours a week, most companies will not pay for benefits. If there is a company policy that part-time positions are not eligible for benefits, you may want to ask if you can continue to receive the full benefits at your own expense.

You should be clear that you expect the same amount of vacation and sick days as with your previous job – adjusted according to your new hours. So if you currently get three weeks (or 15 days) of vacation a year and are shifting to a three-day workweek, then you should propose that your vacation be three weeks times three days, or nine days a year. Take the same approach with sick leave. This will save your employer money, so include it as a cost savings benefit.

Starting your own business requires a more detailed analysis of estimated costs versus revenue projections. Don't forget to include start-up costs – computer, fax machine, letterhead and

Funding your own benefits plan

If you do end up losing your benefits, look for a professional association that offers group benefit plans or check with your alma mater. These plans are generally much cheaper than purchasing individual coverage, even if you have to pay to join the association. Chambers of commerce, boards of trade or trade associations related to your field, whether it's accounting, advertising or manufacturing, may also offer plans.

desk – and estimated monthly business expenses – extra phone line, office rent and couriers. My consulting business costs about $20,000 to $25,000 in office expenses each year and that does not take into account our salaries, marketing costs, professional services (such as our accountant's fees) or any new equipment (such as computers or printers). When looking at revenue expectations, keep in mind that, unless you are running a retail operation, invoices may not be paid for 30 to 60 days. Also make sure you take into account vacation days and sick days, which will impact your ability to generate revenue. Finally, don't forget that you will no longer have health benefits or be eligible for disability pay unless you purchase your own coverage.

Recommend regular performance reviews

Since you are proposing a new and relatively uncertain work arrangement, it's a good idea to meet regularly with your boss or coworkers to check how things are going. Quarterly meetings are a good start. They do not have to include a formal performance review (that can still happen once a year), but they should give you and your boss a chance to talk about how the new arrangement is working out. You might want to recommend specific criteria for evaluation, such as meeting deadlines or juggling multiple projects. Feedback from coworkers is also helpful.

Make sure you set measurable goals that you can review every quarter.

Even if you will be your own boss, you should set specific goals to measure your progress. Make sure you set measurable business goals that you can review every quarter. These can include financial targets, marketing goals or even professional development objectives. Use your team of advisers or your partner to review your performance and help you look at ways to improve the business.

Gather proof that flexible hours work

If you did your homework, you have probably gathered articles, studies or testimonials about women successfully working flexible hours. While this kind of support material is not essential to starting your own business (although it could help inspire and motivate you), it will help convince your employer to say yes to your proposal. Research that extols the benefits of flex policies in the workplace will help educate your employer about the advantages. Be selective with the information you include, however. Your boss can always ask for more details later.

Wrap up with a summary

Don't forget to end your proposal with an upbeat summary of why your boss should seriously consider your proposal. Remind him again of the key skills you have already demonstrated that will ensure your success and how committed you are to making it work. Make sure you also review the benefits of approving your proposal (increased employee loyalty and a restructured, more cost-effective approach to your position, etc.).

If you still find proposal writing daunting, you could look into an excellent resource called Flex Success at www.workoptions.com. For around $39 U.S., you will receive a proposal template to download directly onto your computer. Then all you have to do is fill in the specifics of your situation within the sections provided. Some of the women in this book swore by this product and felt it was instrumental in helping them create a professional proposal and successfully negotiate the work arrangement they wanted.

Start exploring your child-care options

If you don't currently have child care, now is a good time to start looking. While you probably won't want to commit to a child-care arrangement until you have finalized your new work schedule, it takes time to explore child-care options and find the right fit for you and your child.

In particular, it can be hard to find part-time child care or child care that covers flexible hours. Day-care facilities and child-care providers have unfortunately not caught up with women's fast-growing desire to work less than full-time hours…yet! But don't get discouraged. Lots of women are ultimately successful at coordinating part-time care. It just takes an entrepreneurial approach.

Where should you start? To find licensed day-care centers, consult the Yellow Pages or local government offices (some cities, towns or regions offer information for new moms on how to select the right day-care program and where to find one in your area). Few if any sources will tell you how to find a facility that offers part-time or flexible care, so you'll have to call around. There are also thousands of in-home day cares across North America, but they are more difficult to find since they're too small to advertise, except in local newspapers. If you can't find anything through your local paper, scan community center and local business bulletin boards, and ask other women in your neighborhood where they send their kids.

Word-of-mouth is usually the most reliable and cost effective way of finding a caregiver to come to your home. While you may have the good fortune of connecting with a caregiver who already works part time (I did), it is more likely that you will have to find another family willing to share a caregiver and employ her on the days you are not working. That way, together you can hire someone full time. To find other mothers looking for part-time care (or who may have a caregiver they want to shift to part-time hours) put up a notice everywhere these women might look or go – your local newspaper and on the bulletin boards at the local grocery store, church, bank, library, preschools or public schools. One woman I know found a part-time caregiver by asking her son's music teacher to make an announcement in class that she was looking for someone.

From planning to plunging

You've thought it through and now you've got a plan. I'm sure you know what comes next: You have got to take the plunge. If you think back to a risk you've taken in your life – accepting a new job, moving to a new city, getting up in front of an audience – this will likely feel quite similar. You will experience the fear of things not working out (what if your boss doesn't accept your proposal or your business doesn't get off the ground?) and you may lose some sleep.

Just remember that fear can mount like the mercury in a thermometer on a hot summer day until you've taken that first giant step, whether that means meeting with your boss or investing in your new office equipment and business cards. Once you've taken that first step, the mercury will fall, ever so slightly, and will keep falling as you continue along the path to making your vision a reality. Putting it off will only prolong the agony of not knowing whether you can do it or not. I'm willing to bet you can.

CHAPTER 5

Go for It!

"When I pitched the idea of a compressed workweek to my boss, he said: 'What am I going to do without you one day a week?' But we agreed to play it by ear. I was blown away that it went off without a hitch. I think that my willingness to be flexible was key, along with the fact that I went in thinking he's just got to say yes. I'm now doing five days' work in four and I love it. And the company has never made me feel funny about it."

Kimberly is a regional marketing analyst for a life insurance company and the mother of Evan, three, and Drew, 18 months. She negotiated a compressed workweek after being on the job only six months.

This is it! This is your chance to go for what you want and make the flexible work arrangement you've so carefully designed a reality. Most women find this the most difficult step of all – moving on from the planning and proposal stage to actually selling your vision. It takes courage, determination (think of that cute little face smiling up at you) and, above all, a belief that you are entitled to the life you want. You are!

Patricia, the sales promotion manager who redesigned her full-time job into a four-day-a-week position, found it extremely challenging to negotiate a flexible work arrangement while still on maternity leave. Like many first-time mothers, Patricia was feeling fragile and torn at the prospect of reentering the workforce and leaving her baby daughter in a neighborhood day care. She was worried that she would not come across as confident and professional in her pitch to her boss and that she might break down in tears during their discussion. Patricia did make it through the meeting and successfully negotiated a four-day workweek, thanks to a lot of preplanning and consideration of her boss's response.

This is what I call the "preparing yourself for success" stage. For starters, preparing for and practicing your pitch to a boss or prospective employer will be critical to your confidence and success. But equally as important is what you do to prepare yourself and your family for this new work arrangement once it's approved.

Plan your pitch

Whether you've been with your company ten months or ten years, you need to be perfectly clear about why you think this flexible arrangement will work. If you are pitching it to your boss, you have to tailor the information so that he is most likely to say yes. You did some of this thinking when you put together your written proposal, but there are additional things to consider.

If you haven't already broached the subject of a flexible work arrangement with your boss, think carefully about how he likes to receive information. Maybe he likes to know what to expect before he enters a meeting. In that case he may respond better if you tell him why you want to meet with him, before actually pitching your proposal. If your boss seems to handle new information well, or if you think he will be much more likely to hear you out in a face-to-face meeting, then forewarning him may not make sense.

Another important element is timing. Approaching your boss when he is in the midst of annual budget planning or a crunch period is not the wisest move. There may also be a specific day of the week or even time of day that you think he would be most receptive to your proposal. Perhaps speaking with him first thing in the morning, before he is interrupted by other people, makes the most sense. Or you might discuss it over lunch in a less formal setting that relaxes both of you. Think back to when you've asked your boss for something in the past, such as a raise or time off. What approach worked best?

When you're actually pitching your proposal, make sure you position it as a draft. While you need to be strong and confident to make your point, you don't want your boss to think that it's a take-it-or-leave-it proposal (unless, of course, it is). Make sure he understands that it is your best attempt at thinking through all the important aspects of a successful flexible work arrangement. Be clear that you're presenting it for his input and suggestions.

Be confident and let your passion for your proposal shine through.

Be confident. You've worked hard to get to this point, so let your passion for your proposal shine through.

Practice like you would for a job interview

Treat the meeting with your boss as if you were going into a job interview. Practice how you will present the information and how you will answer questions that your boss will likely raise. Even if you think your boss will be receptive to your proposal, it is still important to give it your best shot.

Generally, I find that asking a friend or spouse to role-play your boss works well. Role-playing allows you to practice both your pitch and how you will answer questions on the spot. It might be helpful to provide your friend or partner with a list of questions you anticipate and ask them to make up some of their own. Practicing will accomplish a number of things. It will make you feel more prepared and therefore more confident. It will help you formulate succinct answers to questions instead of rambling on when you're put on the spot during the meeting. Finally, it will help you organize your key arguments for why a flexible arrangement will work for you and the company.

Prepare for objections

While I can honestly say that many of the women I spoke with did not have to deal with many arguments from their bosses, objections do happen. There is no question that developing a detailed proposal and pitching it strategically makes it much more likely that your boss will carefully consider your request. This does not mean, however, that you don't need to cover your bases.

To prepare for objections, think through what your boss would most likely be concerned about and how you will respond in a way that will build up her confidence in your plans. Here are some objections women hear from their supervisors and how you can deal with them:

"We've never done this before."

This is a very common response. There is still a great deal of fear among employers who believe that flexible job arrangements create more work for them, cause more hassles, result in decreased productivity and, most importantly, create performance problems. Most studies on flexible work arrangements (see list of websites on page 61) show quite the opposite. They show evidence that flexible work arrangements make for happier, more motivated employees who are more likely to stay longer at their jobs because they are working the way they want to work.

Another way to deal with this objection is to present positive examples of proposals that have worked. Remind her of times that risks paid off for the company and compare them to your plan. Reiterate to your boss that this arrangement would not be set in stone and that you expect to have a trial period. This may alleviate some of the pressure she's feeling about making a decision that feels final.

"If I let you do this, other employees will want to do it too."

This is an interesting objection given that few employees are ever really treated the same or act the same within a company. Just because one employee takes a one-and-a-half-hour lunch to work out doesn't mean that everyone else will follow suit. Nor does giving a particular employee some time off for working hard mean that every other employee deserves to be similarly compensated.

Furthermore, while many companies currently have employees in flexible work arrangements, the overall number of people working flex hours is still a small percentage of the total workforce – nowhere near the number of full-time workers. Many men and women have no desire to work a more flexible schedule, or there would be more people pushing for it. Finally, the last and probably best argument for approval of your proposal is that it sends a message to all employees that their individual goals are valued.

"Productivity will suffer."

If your boss hits you with this particular objection, she is really saying that she doesn't trust you to get all your work done if she doesn't see you in the office every day. You need to convince her that wherever you're working and whatever hours, you expect to be judged on your performance, not the time you spend in the office. If you don't already set specific annual targets and performance goals with your boss, now would be a good time to suggest setting them. This will help your boss focus on the quality of your work and your contribution to the company, and take the emphasis off how much "face time" you are putting in every week.

"You won't be as accessible."

In Chapter 4 I talked about the difference between being accessible and being available every minute of the day. Even in a full-time office role, we are never completely available to coworkers. Most of us have meetings and appointments, or we need to close our door to meet a deadline. The only real difference with working flexible hours is that there are fewer hours when you are reachable by phone or in your office. You need to show your boss that there are many other ways of being accessible, including e-mail and voice mail, without being a slave to technology. Press upon your boss that you see it as your responsibility to connect with him or your coworkers or clients to ensure that they get what they need from you.

There are many ways of being accessible, including e-mail and voice mail, without being a slave to technology.

"Your job doesn't really lend itself to part-time or flex hours."

This is another common objection, since it is often easy to single out specific responsibilities that don't seem likely to work well within flexible hours. Managing staff or specific clients, approving budgets and major expenses, or working closely with a team can appear difficult to maintain within a flexible work schedule – mostly because face-to-face contact with coworkers or staff seems essential.

Think through which parts of your job might be difficult to handle under a flexible arrangement (hopefully you covered this in your proposal). Then present your boss with viable solutions. These could include having another manager in charge on the day you're not in, setting up a new system for budget approvals or switching some face-to-face team meetings to telephone conferences or e-mail forums.

"My hands are tied; this is not my decision."

A response like this usually means that your boss doesn't want to take on this risk, but also doesn't want to be the one who says no. It's easier for him to pass off responsibility to a "higher power." Try showing your boss that you respect and empathize with the position he is in and offer to take your proposal to the next level so that he doesn't have to. Ask if you should present your proposal to other people in the company who are in a position to make a decision. This kind of subtle pressure will do one of two things: either it will push your boss to make a decision on his own or he will have to let you take it to the next level (unless he's willing to admit that he's the one who is opposed).

Don't rush it

While you may hope that your employer approves your request immediately, it's not realistic to expect instant results. Your boss may want or need you to make your pitch to other people in the company, in particular to his boss. Or he may simply need time to digest your proposal and come back to you with questions or concerns. It's important to balance your desire for resolution with your boss's need to feel comfortable with your proposal. Be prepared to sell others in the company on the value of your proposal and to have further discussions with your boss to ensure that together you've thought of everything.

What will you do when your employer says yes?

When your boss says yes to your flexible work proposal, there is only one thing to do: celebrate! You have worked hard to get to this point and you should revel in the fact that you made this happen. You should also make sure to thank your boss, preferably in writing, for showing confidence in your ability to make the transition to a flexible work arrangement. Reiterate your commitment to making it work. (If your boss says no, don't worry. You do have options – page 97 will give you other suggestions on how to go flex.)

Have you done everything possible to ensure your success?

Congratulations, you are now officially a member of the North American flexible work movement. Now you need to put all the pieces of your plan into action to ensure that you successfully achieve that vision you developed for yourself back in Chapter 2. This means focusing on things such as getting child care in place, thinking through your new schedule and readjusting your spending to reflect your new income (which for most women is a reduction in salary).

Make sure you have lined up the right child care

At this point you should have a good idea of what kind of care you want for your child. You may have already lined up a caregiver or day-care program for your kids. If you are off work on maternity leave, you need to start preparing yourself and your children for the transition into a new child-care setting. If you have a caregiver coming into your home, make sure she starts at least two to three weeks before you go back to work. That way you can get comfortable with how she cares for your children and make sure she has been properly briefed to handle things. If you plan to work from your home, you will need to be very clear with your caregiver about if and when it is all right for her and your children to interrupt you in the office.

The same holds true for day care. Bring your child (or children) to visit the facility a few days a week before you go back to work to help them get used to the environment. This will help alleviate anxiety (theirs and yours) when the time comes. Many day-care programs call this a phase-in period and will recommend how many hours your child will need to get settled.

Before actually switching to your flexible hours, make sure you have found child care or adjusted your current child care to suit your new schedule. It's essential you start your new work arrangement with the comfort and confidence that your children are being well cared for, so that you can put in the hours or days required to make it work.

A word of wisdom from women who've been there: Whatever you do, don't try to wing child care! Unless you have negotiated a completely flexible schedule that allows you to work whatever hours are convenient for you, you will need some kind of child care to cover your work time. One woman I spoke with who has infant children actually had a vision of working out of her home without any other support. She ended up having to put her children in front of the TV most of the day just to get her work done. What's more, she was extremely stressed about not being available to them. A lack of child-care support will only set you up for failure. You've convinced your boss that this new arrangement can work: This is the time to prove it to him. Without proper child care, you run the risk of not delivering on your promises and jeopardizing the arrangement you just negotiated for yourself.

Think through your new schedule

Now that you have successfully negotiated a new work schedule, you should be able to enjoy more time with your children. But you will likely have to rearrange a number of other things in your life to make it work. For instance, if you are shifting to a shorter work day in order to pick up your kids from school or day care by 3:00 p.m., you may have to clear some evenings to complete your work. Or you may not be able to plan scheduled activities with your kids on one of the days you're off due to a monthly departmental meeting you've committed to attend. Whatever the requirements of your new work arrangement, make sure that they are reflected in your weekly schedule. This will avoid conflict and stress – for you and your family.

Another important part of planning your new schedule is working with your partner. You both need to be very clear about who is responsible for what. If you have agreed to share child-care pickup and drop-off, you need to be in sync about who will take which days. If you know there are certain times of the year when you will be busier than others, you may want to line up an emergency care service, neighbor or family member who can fill in when you need extra time to work. I've used two different child-care services to get me through work crunches, and I was glad I had researched and tried them out prior to the actual crunch period. Since I trusted the service and the caregivers they were sending me, I could focus on getting my work done. Emergency care also comes in handy when your child is sick and can't go to day care or school, but you still have to work.

The quicker you adjust your spending to your new income, the less stressed you will be.

Picture what a typical week will look like now. What needs to change to accommodate your new flexible work schedule? Lisa, an organizational development consultant who works out of her home, actually created a weekly schedule with her husband that detailed who was responsible for the children in the mornings and evenings. Since she and her husband work four days each, they share the care of their two children, Skylar, three, and Forrest, 14 weeks. The schedule addresses which days each parent goes into work early and who drops off the kids at day care, which nights each parent is responsible for getting the kids to bed and which nights they will spend as a family. "For some people this kind of scheduling seems way too rigid," says Lisa. "But for us it is very effective and it ensures that my husband and I each have time alone and together, which is very important to us."

Make the necessary financial adjustments immediately

Most women who shift to a flexible work arrangement take a salary cut, which usually equates to a reduction in their household income. Hopefully, you have already figured out how you're going to manage with less money. Now would be the time to start enacting your plan – whether you've decided to renegotiate your monthly mortgage payments, sell one of your family cars or take your lunch to work. The quicker you adjust your spending to your new income, the less stressed you will be about earning less. If you are struggling to understand how you will manage on less money, you may find it helpful to hire a financial planner or an accountant. The right planner can help you develop a long-range plan based on your new flexible work arrangement and your overall financial goals.

Set clear boundaries up front

I don't think that women are particularly good at setting boundaries. We work so hard to please everyone else that we rarely feel comfortable saying no to a friend, spouse or coworker. But working flexible hours requires that you set boundaries. If you don't set up those boundaries in the beginning, you will end up having to do this later. Elizabeth, mother of three-year-old Evelyn, did not set any real boundaries when she accepted her three-day-a-week sales job with a publishing company. As a result, her boss took her commitment to accessibility a little too far. Initially Elizabeth accepted that her boss would call her regularly on her days off, but when he began calling her at night as she was getting her daughter ready for bed, she had to put her foot down. She eventually told her boss that he should only call her at home when it was really important, and she helped him define what she meant by important.

Prepare yourself to say no to most meetings on your days off, to tell people that you can't make a breakfast gathering unless you have lots of notice or to turn down work because you know you are already stretched too thin. None of these are easy things to do. At times you will feel like you are letting people down. You may fear they'll perceive you as not committed to your job or company. Just remember, only you will speak up for you and only you can take charge of making your new flexible arrangement work. So it is up to you to set boundaries for yourself because no one else will.

Get your coworkers on your side

It is never too early to start educating the people you work with about your plan and why you're confident it's going to work. The more coworkers and supervisors who understand what you're trying to do and recognize your effort to make it work, the smoother your transition to flexible work will be. According to Wendy Hirschberg from Ernst & Young, one of the keys to a successful flexible work arrangement is career self-management. "You have to be respectful of your colleagues and comfortable saying, 'These are my limits,'" she says. "You need to take responsibility for communicating regularly and appreciate the fact that your colleagues will often have other things on their mind." Letting coworkers know how you'll stay in touch when you're out of the office, staying connected to team projects and planning regular communications will go a long way in building trust and support for your new work arrangement.

What will you do if your employer says no?

There is a chance that after all of your planning, preparation and pitching, your employer will reject your request to work flexible hours. This will feel like a huge blow after all the trouble you've gone through. Do not automatically assume, however, that you can't reach some kind of compromise.

Buy time

Ask your boss for her specific objections and suggest you go away and think about your discussion and revise your proposal accordingly. If you haven't already done so, it may also be helpful to show your boss examples of success stories in similar companies. If your boss seems dead set against the idea, suggest a trial period of three to six months so that you can show her how it might work. Basically you want to buy yourself some time to figure out your next move.

Try an informal arrangement instead

When Christie, mother of seven-month-old Sam, returned to work after her maternity leave, she found it easier to negotiate an informal arrangement with her boss than making a formal proposal. Nothing was put in writing, so nothing actually had to be approved at a higher level. As a major accounts manager for a packaged goods firm, Christie negotiated working four days in the office and one day at home, without a decrease in salary or bonus. "My boss knew I would get the job done, even if I had to work at night or on weekends," says Christie. While her vision for herself was to work three days a week, she was working in sales for a male-dominated company, so she felt she needed to do it in stages. "I have to work at getting my company to think differently," says Christie.

Since very few companies actually advertise flexible jobs, you'll need to be creative.

"I definitely can see a more flexible schedule happening in the future."

Finding new flexible work opportunities

If you do decide to look for a new job or some other alternative outside your existing company, there are a variety of ways to approach it. Since very few companies actually advertise flexible jobs (most flex arrangements are negotiated by people within a firm), you'll need to be creative. Thirty-five-year-old Suzanne is a wonderful example of how creativity pays off. Suzanne knew once she had her second child that she did not want to go back to the hectic marketing and sales role she had with a publishing company. Mother of four-year-old William and four-month-old Cameron, she had several goals in her search for a new, more flexible position. She wanted to reduce her nearly two-hour daily commute, work four days a week instead of five and manage far fewer staff than she had done in her previous job.

Suzanne applied for positions advertised as full time, but she chose organizations and jobs she thought might be more conducive to a flexible work arrangement. She avoided applying for jobs that required lots of travel, management of a large team of people and a level of responsibility that she intuitively knew would require more hours than she was willing to give. Eventually she landed a marketing position with a not-for-profit organization and negotiated a four-day workweek right from the start. When she got the final job offer, she was ecstatic about achieving her vision and creating a different life for her and her family.

Certain resources can help lead you to companies known for their family-friendly work environment and policies (see page 97). You may also consider taking a contract position. Working on contract generally means that you won't get benefits, but the hourly rate is often higher than a salaried position and there's usually far more opportunity for flexibility. Assuming you can handle the uncertainty of not knowing where your next contract will come from, this option may be for you. You may also be able to create a contract opportunity for yourself by doing work for previous employers or clients. Since you are already a known commodity to them, you may have a greater chance of quickly negotiating something more flexible.

The traditional job hunting approach – talking to anyone and everyone you know – works for flexible work arrangements, too, although you may still have to pursue a full-time position and then try to sell the company on a flexible schedule. Thirty-four-year-old Kimberly, the mother of two who works as a regional marketing associate with an insurance firm, took the job with the intention of negotiating a compressed workweek after she had been there six months. "I thought that six months would give me a chance to get to know the company, and to show them what I could do," says Kimberly.

She knew that she had to put some kind of proposal together, but didn't quite know how to sell it herself. So she did an Internet search and ended up downloading the "Flex Success" blueprint available at www.workoptions.com (highlighted in Chapter 4). "In my proposal, I didn't say, 'It's my way or the highway,'" says Kimberly. "I asked my boss to give me three months to prove myself. I flowed right into it. It was my plan all along. I've now been doing it for seven months and I love it."

Don't expect it to be harmonious right away

Be realistic with your expectations. It's not often that flexible work arrangements work out perfectly from day one. Give yourself

How to find a new flexible work arrangement

- Network, network, network. Ask friends, colleagues and acquaintances whether they know of any flex arrangements.
- Look for work slightly below your skill and salary level. Then sell them on turning a five-day job into four.
- Look for contract work. It is less permanent, but usually offers better hourly rates and more flexible opportunities. Contact previous employers, clients and suppliers for subcontracting opportunities.
- Take a full-time job and renegotiate your hours after six months.
- Research and target family-friendly companies.

Canadian companies

- Canada's Top 100 Employers (order at www.mediacorp2.com – includes ten best employers for women)
- www.frankcommunications.com (somewhat outdated, but the only ever edition of Canada's Best Employers for Women)

U.S. companies

- www.workingmother.com (The 100 Best Companies for Working Mothers)
- www.womans-work.com (lists various flexible work opportunities)

time to get into the swing of working a different schedule and a new mindset now that you're a flexible worker. Realize that no matter how much you try to stay in the loop at work, there will be disappointments. You may find out your boss didn't ask you to be part of a really exciting project because she didn't think you could meet the deadline. Or you missed an important company announcement because it was made on your day off. You may even find, after being at it for a few weeks or months, that the schedule you've designed for yourself is not working out quite as well as you'd hoped. Expect to adjust and revise your arrangement once you have had a chance to actually live it.

While your situation may not be perfect, the hardest part is over. You have successfully secured a flexible arrangement and you are on the road to achieving a better balance in your work and your family life. The only thing to do now is to savor it.

CHAPTER 6

Taking One Foot Off the Career Track

"When I began working three days a week on contract, I lost all my benefits and became the lowest person on the totem pole. But instinctively I knew that this would be less stressful than having to choose between a full-time job and my daughter. I still have a sense of being a career woman. I enjoy being with colleagues and bringing in an income. And I also get to be a mommy. If it means changing jobs every year, then that's what I'll do. There's just so much more to life than working five days a week."

Rita, a hospital administrative technician, is the mother of two-year-old Olivia.

When you trade work hours for time with your children, you are essentially making a new career choice for yourself. Most likely, your priorities have shifted, and your focus on your work is inevitably affected. That's not to say that women who work flexible hours can't get promoted or move ahead. In fact, many women successfully advance in the workplace even though they have cut back on their work hours. It just takes them a little longer to reach their goal than they had originally anticipated. But, as most women who have made the transition to flexible work will tell you, there is no getting around the fact that working fewer hours or a flexible schedule usually means taking one foot off the career or job track.

Pat Brown from First Tennessee Bank urges women to be honest with themselves about the choices they're making. "If being at home with your baby is important to you, then stepping off the career track or altering your job should be okay," says Pat. "You have to come to terms with who you are now, what you want and what's important. And at some point you have to realize that you can't have it all."

My shift from being a full-time working woman to a part-time working mother put me in a completely new category.

When I took one foot off I felt like I'd lost my place in society. Because my identity was no longer anchored to a full-time career, I struggled with what to say to people when they asked what I did. Was I a part-time self-employed consultant, or a mother of one who worked part time? Was it a bad thing to tell people that I didn't work full time or was it important to put a stake in the ground and be clear that my life was a delicate balance of working and being a mom?

My shift from being a full-time working woman to a part-time working mother put me in a completely new category. I no longer felt like I belonged to the full-time working crowd, but I also didn't fit in with stay-at-home mothers because I worked. When I'd chat with other mothers who worked full time, I found myself trying to overstate the importance of my work or the number of hours I was actually working at the time. When I'd run into stay-at-home moms in my neighborhood, I would make sure they knew I was home with my son two days a week (especially if they mentioned having run into him recently with his caregiver). Most of the time, I still feel like I am straddling a median strip on a highway. I don't really belong on either side of it. And while this can be a lonely place, I have eventually come to realize that straddling the median is where I can best achieve my own vision and sense of balance.

Many other women echo my feelings. This is part of the identity transformation that you too will likely go through. With time, you will realize that you're not alone (consider all the women in this book). You just need to give yourself a few months to settle into your new arrangement and the new you.

Getting in touch with the new you

If you feel your identity is being challenged, don't panic. Understand that this is a direct result of the change you have just made or are about to make. Think about it. For the last five to 15 years, you have been working full time. The kind of work or positions you held have defined who you are. Now you've discovered another very important calling – motherhood – and your focus must be split between your job and your role as a mom.

What can you expect? Most women say they feel out of their element. It's somewhat like learning to drive a car. At first it feels kind of awkward to sit behind the wheel with all of these strange controls and a whole new set of rules before you. You try to calm your nerves by telling yourself you'll do just fine, but that doesn't stop you from doubting whether you can really master it. You worry about hitting other cars, finding the brake when you're going down a hill or (as in my case) failing the parallel parking test. (It took me three tries!) Changing your work arrangement is unnerving at best, but like driving, once you've been at it awhile, it will begin to feel like second nature.

For Cynthia, the single mother who traded in a high-profile health-care job to start her own publishing business in a rural community, it took months to deal with stepping off the career track. "My identity was wrapped up in my title," says Cynthia. "Moving from a large urban center to a rural community where I wear red rubber boots to work some days also took some adjusting to. I found my friends' reactions to the change interesting. One friend actually asked me, 'What's that going to do to your résumé?' But I can honestly say today that there's no turning back for us. I intend to keep building on the flexibility I've established."

This identity transformation you're going through is in essence forcing you to come to terms with the new you. You need to give yourself permission to accept and appreciate the person you are becoming. In other words, it's all right to want to work less and postpone getting a promotion, if that's what it takes to achieve a balance between work and motherhood.

Worrying about your future job prospects

You are probably very worried right now about how a flexible work arrangement will affect your career or job prospects to come. I wish I could tell you that the careers of all the women who have chosen to work flexible hours have stayed on track. But I don't think you'd really believe me. Working flexible hours will likely have an impact on your career in some way, but remember it's up to you to decide what kind of impact you are comfortable with. The type of arrangement you choose, or have already chosen, will determine whether you continue on the career path you pursued before you had children, slow it down or change its direction altogether.

When I shifted to a three-day workweek, I was very conscious that I was not only giving up two days of income each week, but I was also temporarily abandoning my dream of expanding our business into a larger consulting practice. And I have to admit there are days that owning a two-person consulting firm doesn't feel all that successful to me. In addition, I have had to play more of a background role (instead of being an equal partner) in the business because I work fewer hours and am in my home office more (to stay close to Zachary) rather than meeting with clients. This means that I often work on less interesting projects and have more limited learning and career growth opportunities than my husband. Translation: Vince takes on all the interesting stuff and receives all the client recognition, too.

Most women worry about how their new work arrangement will influence their potential to work full time in the future. I suggest that women who are struggling with this issue turn the equation around and think about this: Keeping one foot on the career track will make it that much easier for you to return to full-time work in the future. Whether you are running your own business or working part time for someone else, you are still connected to your work and the workforce. This means that if you do decide to go back full time at some point, you won't have to reorient yourself. Your skills, contacts and knowledge of the workplace will remain current, and even though you may have slowed down your career, you are still gaining valuable experience for the future.

Mary Lynne worked reduced hours when her children were young and has since made the transition back to full-time work. She and her husband were both working in advertising when they had their two boys, who are now 12 and 13. Tired of a one-hour daily commute, working crazy hours and not seeing enough of her children, Mary Lynne approached her employer about job sharing. They turned her down. Within six months, she left the company and formed an ad agency with her husband, which they ran out of their home.

When her boys were young, Mary Lynne worked up to five hours a day (including during the kids' naps) and spent the rest of the day with her children. "I always wondered whether it was possible to have a fulfilling career, like what I was doing and still enjoy my kids while they were young," she says. "I've definitely achieved these objectives." Today she works full time, and she and her husband have a thriving 13-person firm outside of their home. They are gradually selling the business to their employees.

Probably the most important thing that you can do to leave the door open for future full-time work is to stay connected with colleagues. Take time to nurture relationships with clients and colleagues if you run your own business, or coworkers and managers if you're working for a company. Wendy Hirschberg from Ernst & Young believes that these very relationships are most important to your success. She recommends that women should make time for relationship-building once they have a better handle on their new flexible work arrangement.

So while you will undoubtedly feel pressured to work through lunch at your desk or to pass on attending a daylong seminar, don't make the mistake of cutting yourself off completely. Make sure you arrange lunches with colleagues and attend industry events at least a few times a year. And don't forgo company retreats or important client functions, even if they occur on your days off.

Feeling less connected to your work

One of the most significant challenges women face when they switch to flexible work is that they feel like they are no longer on top of everything at work. Reducing your hours or changing the way you work obviously makes it more difficult to be as connected to your job, your colleagues and what's going on at the office as you were before. Many women report feeling out of the loop or forgotten because they aren't as visible in the office as they once were. Other women find that it requires too much energy and time to try to stay as involved as when they were working full time. Face it, if you've shifted to a three-day-a-week position, you can't possibly expect to have as much time to socialize with colleagues, attend meetings or get involved in as many projects as you once did. It is natural to feel cut off or left out.

For your own peace of mind, you'll need to let go of being in the loop.

If you can begin to accept that this is a natural outcome of the transition you are making, in six to 12 months it won't feel so strange anymore. For your own peace of mind, you'll need to let go of being in the loop. Remember Sophie, who works three days a week as a communications project manager in the financial services sector? When she went from a full-time to part-time position, she found that she no longer had as good a grasp on the bigger picture. "I really do have limited knowledge of what else is going on in my department and within the company," says Sophie. "I often don't attend divisional meetings because of my three-day schedule, so I really only know what I'm working on. I've accepted that I don't have time anymore to know everything. I made a choice and I like the flexibility I get from working part time."

You also need to devise ways of staying connected to the stuff that really matters. Some women do this by asking a coworker to copy them on all pertinent e-mails, memos and other important information they might miss if they're not in the office. If you run your own business you need to be clear with clients about staying connected within the structure of your schedule. Think about ways to keep yourself in the loop without having to be available every day.

Letting yourself slow down

As women, we are used to making sacrifices for the ones we love, but we are not used to deliberately sabotaging our own career plans. This is strong language, but taking one foot off the career track often feels exactly like sabotage. Essentially you are trying to slow down for a while or even for an indefinite period of time. You're going to have to come to terms with what will happen to the work you currently do, the career track you may have been on and the professional goals you had set.

Changing to a more flexible work schedule may require you to give up certain responsibilities you enjoyed or the chance to earn a position you once coveted. You may even have to agree to a less challenging job or work for a company that offers fewer opportunities. This can make you feel anxious, like you have given up too much. Remember you can't have it all and slowing down is almost always a necessary trade-off to getting what you want: more time with your kids. Try listing everything you've gained from making the switch to flexible work. At the very least, this will help reconfirm why you've made these choices for yourself and your family.

Take Elizabeth, for example, the mother who works three days a week in a sales job with a publishing company. Prior to taking the part-time position with a new firm, Elizabeth actually turned down the opportunity to return to the company where she had worked before her daughter was born. She gave up a higher-profile, more lucrative sales position to maintain a balance between work and family. "At first my identity felt so battered, but now I feel like I've got myself back," she says. "I'm not wholly satisfied with the job I'm in, but I know that if I want to go further, I'm going to have to go full time. For now, I love the fact that I get to spend time with my daughter while keeping one foot on the career track."

Feeling guilty about not working hard enough

Just about every woman I know is familiar with guilt. So it's not surprising that women who shift to flexible work experience great pangs of guilt for not being in the office enough or not putting in the kind of effort they used to. It's completely normal to feel like you are letting your boss or coworkers down when you have to say no to an assignment or a team project. For many of us, the hours we put in have become a symbol of how hard we work. So when we reduce those hours, we simply don't feel as committed as we once were. And the truth is, most of us don't want to be!

In my case, I found it extremely difficult in the beginning to tell a client that I wasn't going to be in on Monday or Friday of each week. In fact it made me so uncomfortable that for the first year I never really admitted that I was working only three days a week. I simply told clients that I had other client commitments or was out of the office at meetings. This meant that I was constantly checking my voice mail for anything urgent I would need to deal with that day. After a while I realized clients rarely needed to speak with me the same day they left their message. I also worked to convince myself that there was nothing wrong with saying I didn't work full time. Now I make sure that all my clients know when I am in the office and when I am off. That way there's no confusion and I don't feel pressured to pretend I'm working when I'm not.

Another thing I learned was not to be so hard on myself. You'll need to practice this, too! Give yourself permission to work less or be less available if that's what your new work schedule is designed to help you do. You have different priorities now. That doesn't mean that work is less important to you than it was before; it's simply no longer the only priority. And that's okay. Don't judge your performance by the hours you keep. Judge it by how well you're meeting the new personal and work goals you set for yourself.

Thirty-one-year-old Theresa, a human resources adviser for a utilities company, knows all about taking one foot off the career track to spend more time with her children. After her son Jared was born, she negotiated going back to work four days a week. She knew when she asked to work reduced hours that people would see her as less committed than before. "The people who do well in my company work long hours," says Theresa. "I'm definitely off the career track because I'm not the overly committed employee anymore. When I first made the switch to four days, this felt like such a big weight to carry. How was I going to deal with not being as invested as I was before? Now I fully admit and accept that I don't go the extra mile. I've learned that you need to keep your life simple."

The other thing you must carefully avoid is falling into the trap of overcompensating to cope with your guilt. Don't let a successfully negotiated three- or four-day workweek become a five-day reality. The last thing you want to do is work more than you've negotiated. If you do, this will say two things to your employer: One, that you really weren't serious about working a more flexible schedule; and two, that you're willing to do more work for less money than before. Treat your new arrangement as you would a brand new job. Set new parameters for what you can handle and achieve. That way your boss and colleagues will know what to expect from you early on.

Dealing with a change in how you're perceived

Many women who make the shift to more flexible work find that their family and friends start treating them differently. Kathleen, a mother of two young girls, Melissa, five, and Emily, six, runs a landscaping company with her husband. As soon as she shifted to a three-day workweek her mother perceived her to have all kinds of free time. "When there was some errand that needed doing, she would look to me to do it," says Kathleen. "She would say to my siblings, who all work full time, Kathleen's not working so she can pick up that gift at Sears."

Don't let the attitudes of others influence how you feel about your new arrangement.

As soon as you announce that you are shifting to a more flexible work schedule, you are suddenly viewed as less committed and less interested in your career. Your boss and coworkers may question your dedication to your work and to the company, while friends and family members may not view you as the career woman they once did. The most significant challenge is not letting the attitudes of others influence how you feel about your new arrangement. This is not easy, but I guarantee the more comfortable and confident you are in your new role, the less you will be affected by the perceptions of people around you. Your confidence will also go a long way in swaying skeptics that you are serious about making this work.

Just ask Georgina, a corporate immigration lawyer for a large firm. Right after adopting her daughter, she became pregnant with her son. With two babies only eight months apart, she approached her firm about working four days a week. As a result of her shift to a four-day workweek, two of the firm's partners barely speak to her. She has been accused of "dabbling in law," even though her part of the practice turned a profit while she was on maternity leave. "There is an attitude here that I am less professional because I work four days a week," says Georgina. "It's too bad that optics are so important and you have to be 'seen' coming in at 7:00 a.m. or leaving at 10:00 p.m. to be considered committed. The reality is that I can do my job from just about anywhere and fortunately my clients realize this and have been very supportive. I have let go of the fear of being fired. I know my value and I make sure that my supervisor does, too."

You may also experience resentment from colleagues after you shift to a more flexible schedule. Some coworkers may think you are getting "special treatment," while others may worry about having to pick up some of the slack because you're not working full time. You need to show them that this is not the case and that while you may need to rely on them at times, you will be available to return the favor. Build their confidence by looking for opportunities to help coworkers out of a jam. If you're going out of your way to help others, they will be more likely to be sympathetic when you can't make a deadline or a meeting. And speaking of deadlines, make sure you give plenty of notice when you're going to miss one. That way coworkers will be less likely to blame it on your new work arrangement.

Create a formal feedback mechanism with your boss and coworkers via e-mail or regular meetings. It shows that you care about how the arrangement is working for them. It also gives you an opportunity to suggest ways they might work better with you and ensure you are meeting their expectations. And don't be afraid to toot your own horn within reason, of course. Show the people you work with that you still take great pride in your work.

Feeling like you've lost some independence

Many women report that shifting to a flexible work schedule results in an increase in both child-care and household responsibilities (since they're at home more). While this is nothing to fear, it may make you feel like you have lost some of the freedom and independence you had as a full-time working woman.

For starters, with a full-time job your time at work isn't completely your own but you can go grab a coffee if you want, run an errand or go out for lunch. On the days you're home with your children, you won't have the same flexibility (welcome to the life of a stay-at-home mom). You may also find that your spouse's expectations of you have changed as a result of your less hectic work schedule. While you are probably quite accustomed to managing the household and running errands for your family, you may find that he expects you to take on more of those chores now that your work schedule is reduced.

One night I had dinner with a couple; the wife worked two and a half days a week. The husband said openly that he expected his wife to have dinner on the table when he arrived home after work, even though they used to share this responsibility. I got the impression she felt this was not always reasonable, given that it sometimes cut into her time with their children.

Additional issues can arise when you trade some of your income for more flexibility and your contribution to the total household income drops. Many women find it difficult to have their work come second to their spouse's just because they're not putting in the hours they used to or making the money they once did. Coming second can mean that you're the one expected to sacrifice your work day when your kids are sick or put your work on hold when your husband has to work late or go out of town.

Sometimes you have to sacrifice what seems steady and safe in order to create a better balanced life.

All of these things can make you feel like you've lost some of your independence. This can be scary and for many women it feels like a step in the wrong direction (how many years have we been fighting for equality and independence?). The trick is to ensure that you're not taking on so many new household duties that you can't enjoy this extra time you have carved out to be with your kids. You need to communicate with your spouse about what is reasonable for you to take on. Be honest and open with him, and you stand a much better chance of being truly happy in your new arrangement.

Chances are you'll be grateful you took one foot off

While I can't guarantee that switching to a flexible work arrangement will be right for you, I do know that most women who have made this change are very happy with their decision. As you have seen in this chapter and perhaps your own experience, the challenges are many but so are the rewards.

For all the insecurity and guilt you may feel, you should also feel a growing appreciation for the wonderful moments you will have with your children. For all the times the demands of your boss will conflict with those of your children, you will learn new and better ways to manage a flexible schedule that works for you. And for all the worrying you will do about the future and your career prospects, you will experience the incredible rewards of working and being a hands-on mom.

So go ahead and take one foot off. And remember that sometimes you have to be willing to sacrifice what seems steady and safe in order to create a better balanced life in the long run.

CHAPTER 7

Juggling Your Two Worlds

"When my husband and I first started our business out of our home, we integrated our work with whatever was going on in the household. If I needed to concentrate, I would do the work at night. The kids were afraid of the phone because every time it rang they were told to be quiet. On the other hand they also had a sense that there was always one parent there for them. Running our own business from home around our sons' schedules added more things to our life to juggle. But I think we're pretty close because of it."

Mary Lynne is the mother of two who has been running an advertising agency with her husband for more than ten years.

When you enter into a flexible work arrangement, you are moving toward a more flexible life overall. You have actively pursued flexibility in your work hours; now you'll find that you have to be more flexible in other areas of your life as well. Many women with flexible hours talk about getting used to their two worlds colliding and the stress of constantly being pulled back and forth between work mode and motherhood mode. This tug-of-war between work responsibilities and time with your children is bound to happen, and the more flexible your work schedule, the more likely you will experience it. This chapter will help you get more comfortable with juggling, so you can start enjoying your new arrangement.

While writing this book, I've found that my two worlds have become more intertwined than ever before. Before Zachary turned three, my set-up was more structured. I had an in-home caregiver three days a week, which meant I always knew which three days I would work. All of this changed when Zachary started going to preschool Monday, Wednesday and Friday mornings, and my caregiver came two days a week (Tuesdays and Thursdays). My work time and my time with Zachary has become much more fragmented: I work mornings when he's at school, during naps and on the two days our caregiver is here. As a result I find myself frantically banging off e-mails to clients at 11:55 a.m. when I'm due to pick him up from school at noon, or rushing back to the office to call a client after putting him down for his afternoon nap. I had to learn to switch my work hat with my mom hat, or vice versa, in a matter of minutes. There are times when I really have to juggle to get enough uninterrupted time with Zachary to just be in the moment, whether we're baking banana muffins or building a block tower.

Gaining flexibility in your work arrangement means that you are buying into a dynamic, ever-changing lifestyle. On the one hand, you get to go on your child's school trip or spend a morning making sand castles at the park. On the other hand, you need to be willing to step out of your agreed-upon work schedule occasionally to meet the demands of your job or business. Let's say you negotiate working Mondays, Wednesdays and

Fridays so that you can spend Tuesdays and Thursdays with your child. You need to be open to the fact that there will be Tuesdays or Thursdays when you need to go into the office to participate in a quarterly departmental meeting or put in extra work hours to meet a deadline.

If your job has seasonal ups and downs, then you may need to work additional hours during a certain time of the year. Carolyn, a partner at an accounting firm, negotiated a flexible work schedule when her first child was born by agreeing to work full time for three months during audit season and part time (three days a week) the rest of the year. Carolyn, who is now the mother of three boys, Kenny, ten, Bobby, seven, and Billy, two, remembers how challenging it was to be the first employee in a client-service role in her firm to work reduced hours. "I remember that some partners would call a meeting at five o'clock and I would have a knot in my stomach because I knew I had to leave at 5:30 to pick up my son," says Carolyn. "I also found that while I was supposed to work the same three days every week, I often had to change my schedule to accommodate my workload. But I would rather do the juggle than not be there with my kids."

Once you get the swing of your new work arrangement, you will appreciate your newfound flexibility more than anything.

Regardless of the schedule you've negotiated for yourself, there will be times when you will have to do some significant juggling to make it work. This juggling can make you feel stretched and guilty about not being able to give your child or your work your undivided attention. You may even go so far as to question why you set up this arrangement in the first place. Whatever you're feeling, rest assured that this is simply another important step in your transition to creating a better life for yourself and your family. While you may feel that things are rough in the beginning, once you get the swing of your new work arrangement, you will appreciate your newfound flexibility more than anything.

Let go of unrealistic expectations

Good jugglers never have too many balls in the air at once. To let go of some of these balls, you need to let go of your unrealistic expectations about what you should be able to accomplish under your new flexible work arrangement.

Almost all women, and mothers in particular, seem to have unrealistic expectations for themselves. And a funny thing happens when you make the shift to flexible work. On the one hand, you still think you should be working just as hard and producing the same results as when you worked full time. On the other hand, now that you have more time with your children you think you should be able to do all the important mothering jobs you may not have had time for before. While you've finally come to accept you can't have it all, you may find that you still expect yourself to do it all.

For example, you may expect to continue with a training program at work, which may not be doable now that you're working three days instead of five. Or you may pressure yourself to spend every available minute stimulating your children, when you need to give yourself permission to check your e-mail or set up a meeting on an afternoon you were supposed to go to the zoo.

Suzy, a self-employed communications consultant and mother of Nicholas, four, and Alex, two, felt pressured to make nutritious meals every night for her children – just like her mother did. "There is no question I feel guilty about things like not making more nutritious meals for my kids or spending less time with them than their caregiver does," says Suzy. "I definitely cut corners around the home to make this work, but I'm happy with the choices I've made. At least I live my life on my own terms."

For my part, I've had to let go of running from my office every time Zachary scrapes his knee or bumps his head. I realized when we moved our office into our home that I expected to be his full-time comforter, even though we had a very loving caregiver who was responsible for playing that role three days a week. I had to readjust that expectation and give myself permission to be unavailable on the days when I was working. Although I still try to take a few minutes to be with him on the days he's not feeling well or having a bad day, when I've got a deadline to meet I try to let his cries go.

It's not always easy to identify what's not working at first. The best way to do this is to be aware of what stresses you. If you find that you are sweating by the time you sit down to dinner because you're trying to make a meal from scratch each night, it's okay to order in or buy some ready-made dinners that require little preparation. If you feel pressured to bathe your children every night even though you find the routine exhausting, then give yourself a break and try doing it every other night. Maybe your husband can take over the laundry. Maybe you need to take a hiatus from volunteering at the church. Try going back to your vision and reviewing your objectives; compare them against how you're actually spending your time. Then create some new expectations for yourself – ones that are more in line with who you are now and what you can realistically accomplish.

Just do your best

Learning to accept what you can realistically accomplish means realizing you cannot always give your all to your work or your kids. This is the reality of flexible work. Constantly shifting your focus back and forth between mothering and work makes it difficult to feel like you're fully dedicated to either. You may find that there are times when you simply can't separate the two. Catherine, a professional trainer, knows the stress of trying to meet her work commitments while still being available to her 14-month-old daughter, Kaleigh. Catherine says it is not uncommon for her to be up on a stool in the middle of her living room practicing her presentation for the next day in front of her daughter.

This is the reality of flexible work. Constantly shifting your focus back and forth between mothering and work.

Like Catherine, many of us are mothers and part-time workers and we need to accept – better yet embrace – the fact that we can't expect to do either job perfectly all of the time. This does not mean that you can't do a good job as a worker or a mother. It simply means that all you can do is your best and that your best should be good enough.

Kathleen, the mother who runs a landscaping business with her husband, found herself worrying that people might question her commitment to her career when she made the shift to part-time work. When her daughters, Melissa and Emily, were young, she would strap them in their car seats and take them with her to people's homes where she would cut the grass and tend the gardens. "I was worried that people questioned my dedication to work because I had my kids in the truck with me when I was working," says Kathleen. "I worried about this even though I knew that I had chosen for that to happen."

Women with flexible work arrangements will tell you that your work hours and your time with your kids will ebb and flow. This means that no two weeks will probably ever be the same and that you should expect to be more focused on work sometimes and more focused on your baby at others.

Try cutting yourself some slack. Take the advice of Joanne, the successful business owner and author: "I've come to realize that there is a lot of joy surrounding the attempt to find balance. There are always going to be huge screw-ups, so you need to have a sense of humor to live with the chaos. And you need to take your guilt off the hook and realize that you are doing the best you possibly can."

Remember you're in charge

When you're struggling to make your new flexible work arrangement come together, it's easy to forget that you are in charge. Remember you were the one who envisioned a new life for yourself. You successfully negotiated what you wanted. Now it's up to you to make it work – whether that means learning how to let go of guilt or come up with solutions to your work/family conflict.

One good way to take charge is to discipline yourself about your time. To be successful you must motivate yourself to stay on track with your work, without letting it eat into your time with your children. Part of working more independently and more flexibly may mean having to push yourself to work at non-traditional times of the day, including in the morning before your kids get up or at night after they're in bed. Since Zachary was born, my husband and I have had to put in a number of workdays on the weekend because we couldn't get our work done and the weekend was the only time I could line up an extra day of child care. I could motivate myself to put in these extra hours because I was disciplined about making sure I got quality time with Zachary during my days off.

Some women have to discipline themselves in the other direction. You may have to learn how to turn off the cell phone when you are with your kids or stop yourself from checking e-mail every half hour when you're home. You may even need to set up a system for yourself that makes it more difficult for you to give into work when you're with your children. One woman I spoke with actually resorted to signing up for a morning class with her daughter a few times a week to make sure she got out of the house and away from work. It's not easy to admit that we might need incentives to help us enjoy our time with our children. But if that's what it takes for you to pull yourself away from work, then go for it!

Another thing to remember is that only you can control the extra hours you put in or the way you respond to a boss's or coworker's request. Technically, no one will ever force you to work extra hours or attend a meeting on your day off. The pressure you feel to do these things is probably mostly from within, so you need to take charge of how you respond to these requests. I have found that the more comfortable I am being honest with clients about what I can and can't deliver, the more in control I feel of my time and the less conflict I feel between my work and mothering roles.

Set limits. Say no.

Women are not particularly good at saying no, and yet this is a skill you must embrace to make your flexible schedule work.

Part of saying no is separating what's important to you, such as meeting work commitments and spending a morning at the park with your daughter, from what you think you should be doing – everything for everyone.

Having flexibility means that you are often working different hours than other people in your office or telling clients that you're not available at certain times. This often means having to say no – no to a meeting on a day that you spend with your children, no to taking on another project when your three days a week have already turned into four or no to your child when you simply can't be home to help her with a school project.

When I started being honest with clients about my schedule and more realistic with myself about deadlines, I reduced my anxiety tremendously. In fact, it's working so well that clients actually notice when they find me in on a day I'm supposed to be off. Once when I was in the office and took a call from a client on a Friday, the first thing she said was, "Hey! What are you doing in the office today? Isn't this your day with Zachary?"

Of course, saying no to work is challenging enough, but saying no to your kids can be brutal. Children – even small ones – pick up on the fact that you are home certain days of the week or available to pick them up from school on a certain afternoon. Telling them that you have to go in to work at a time usually scheduled for them can be very difficult for you and for them.

Fern, a self-employed lawyer and mother of three boys, ages one to eight, knows all about saying no to her children. Fern made the transition from working in a high-profile law firm to running her own practice so she would have more time for her family. While Fern enjoys the freedom of spending time with her sons – whether it's a local mom-and-tot class on a weekday morning or an afternoon soccer match – she is often challenged when her work time cuts into her mom time.

Fern remembers when two of her sons went off for their first day of summer camp and she promised to meet them at the bus stop later that day. She got caught up in the office with a client project, which took much longer than she had anticipated. As the day wore on and she realized that she wasn't going to keep her promise, she felt more and more anxious. "At some point I had to accept that I wasn't going to see my sons get off the bus," says Fern. "Then I reminded myself that I had spent the entire week before camp hanging out with them." Fern says she now understands that there will always be times she has to say no. "I hope there are enough times I say yes that they see that I'm really trying," she adds.

Getting comfortable with saying no is all about making conscious decisions about what's really important. On some days that will be your work and on other days it will be your kids. The trick is to find the right balance between the two.

Be ruthless with your time

While you may feel like your prioritization skills have already been put to the test, be prepared to become an expert. Shifting to a flexible work schedule makes it essential. There are only so many hours in a week and you can't invent more, but you can get better at putting the important stuff first.

When I first began running my own business, before I became a mom, I was ruled by to-do lists. Pretty much everything on the list got done (even if it took months for me to get to it). So it's not surprising that I was in the office an average of six days a week and running around town doing errands on the seventh!

After I had Zachary and reduced my work hours, I knew I had to become ruthless with my time. I started cutting things out that I had not yet been able to let go. I stopped adding everything to my in-basket. I narrowed my reading list down to only two industry publications. I began saying no to suppliers who wanted to meet with me just to tell me about their firm. I asked them to send me some information instead and filed it for future reference. Before taking on urgent projects, I learned to give first priority to work I had already accepted, even if that meant turning clients down. I even made a list of priority people (and not-so-priority people) that I wanted to see more often. To this day my sister-in-law jokes with me about whether or not she's still on "the list." I know she's got a list, too.

Accept that some items on your list will simply never get done and make smart decisions with the time available to you.

Being ruthless is about two things: accepting that some items on your list will simply never get done and making smart decisions with the time available to you. You'll suddenly have to decide whether you actually have time to have lunch with a colleague or attend a departmental meeting – things you once took for granted. If you work out of your home, you'll be faced with telling your mother you can't talk on the phone about the latest family crisis (your father forgot to tell your uncle about the family barbecue next month) because you're in the middle of a deadline. Or your fridge will break down and you'll have to decide whether to call the repairman immediately or wait until you get that fax sent off to your boss.

It's all part of juggling. The more experienced you get at it, the easier it will be to keep all the important balls in the air.

Change what's not working

Of course all the juggling in the world won't fix what's not working. Many women find that once they start living their new flexible work arrangement, things aren't coming together exactly as they had hoped. Let's face it, you have embarked on a brand-new adventure and while you had a picture of how it would all turn out, you know that life rarely delivers exactly what you envisioned. Maybe you'll discover that you can't possibly get your kids off to day care and still make it to the office by 8:30, so you need to readjust your work hours accordingly. Or perhaps you'll find that even though you're clear with coworkers that you can't take calls most Fridays, people are nonetheless calling with urgent requests. Some women find that their new child-care arrangement isn't meshing with their new work schedule or that while their boss agrees to a four-day-workweek, he hasn't pared down any of their responsibilities from five days.

So what do you do when things don't unfold the way you planned? Figure out what's wrong and change it. While it may take you a while to pinpoint exactly what's not working for you, as soon as you do you should act on it. You may need to sit down with your boss again and offer solutions on how to reorganize your workload. Or perhaps you'll have to enlist outside help to get your kids to school every morning. The quicker you make the necessary changes, the sooner you will be living your vision.

Alicia found out the hard way that working at home without formal child care wasn't for her. A full-time financial business administrator and mother of Christopher, six, and Alexa, two-and-a-half, Alicia negotiated working two days a week from home, but didn't set up child care for Alexa on the days she was home working. "Once I get my son to school, I basically have to put my daughter in front of the television so I can get my work done," says Alicia.

"I try hard not to take any phone work home so I can at least do some of my paperwork sitting at a table with her while she does a puzzle, but it's very difficult. I had this picture of my daughter entertaining herself but I didn't really think about the fact that I'd be trying to put in an eight-hour day. It's definitely not working." After working this way for three months Alicia was trying to line up child care for the days she worked at home.

Remember, this flexible arrangement is your baby! Don't be afraid to try to make it better, because the better it works for your employer and your family, the happier you will be.

Park your guilt

Even if you do set up the most perfect flexible work arrangement, there will still be times when your guilt won't let you enjoy it. I don't know a single woman who could say that she is completely guilt free. The good news is that you can minimize your guilt substantially by following these steps: readjust your expectations of yourself, prioritize, let go of things and set limits.

Focusing on what actually makes me feel guilty is the only way I can eliminate or at least reduce my guilt. My biggest guilt trip probably comes when I am working longer hours and not getting enough quality time with Zachary. I know he senses my increased busyness, my reduced patience level and the fact that we just aren't connecting like we normally do. I can see it in his behavior toward me – lots of power struggles. In times like these I try to do two things. First I consciously accept that there will always be busy work times during the year and that this is okay because I can take chunks of time with Zachary at other times of the year. Then I look at how I can carve out some time with him right away and try to reconnect. I put off all errands and take the time to do things he really likes. This helps me slow down and it shows him that I really want to spend time with him alone.

You can't expect to achieve that perfect balance between work and mother-hood every day.

Of course it's unrealistic to avoid all errands on the days you're with your kids. Life goes on and things like doctor's appointments, grocery shopping and buying new running shoes need to get done. The trick is to not let yourself feel guilty when you try to cross a few things off your to-do list on a nonwork day. If your kids are old enough you might try making your errands or household chores fun. Zachary and I play "I spy" when we're doing the groceries and I can keep him busy and content cleaning just about anything if I give him a cloth and a bucket of water. Or maybe simply carving up your time into a focused half hour of playtime and then an hour of errands will help you feel more balanced.

You can't expect to achieve that perfect balance between work and motherhood every day. You should take a more long-term perspective when evaluating your flexible work arrangement. Look at how you are balancing your work and your time with your children over a three- or six-month period. Hopefully you will see that you are in fact achieving a good balance overall, which should help alleviate some of the guilt you feel on a daily or weekly basis.

When juggling becomes second nature

Eventually the juggling does become easier. For many women it becomes so ingrained in their lives that it feels like second nature. Lanice, the family doctor and mother of three, has been juggling for more than 12 years. She has done everything from working emergency department shifts and filling in part time for other doctors to running her own practice, where she now works an average of three and a half days a week. "It's the best of all worlds," says Lanice. "Sure there was guilt when my children were really little and I'd have these moments where I thought a really good doctor would be at work right now. But the one thing I've learned is that the more I compartmentalize my life, the more I keep my two worlds separate, the better it works for me. I try to live in the moment. So when a patient is telling me a story, I need to listen and not be thinking about what I'm going to make for dinner that night. I don't feel guilty anymore. I feel blessed."

CHAPTER 8

You Did It!

"When I put together the list of what I wanted in my new work arrangement, I expected to give in on some of those things. Working four days a week wasn't the deal-breaker, but the picture of it had settled in my head. I'm glad that I mentioned it up front in my job interview. I guess in a way I was digging my feet in, and it worked. I feel like I got everything I wanted. It feels too good to be true."

Suzanne is the mother who negotiated a four-day workweek in her new role as director of communications and marketing for a charity.

The best part about meeting women who have created a flexible work arrangement for themselves is seeing how thrilled they are with their own success. While no woman will tell you that working flexible hours has given her everything she hoped for, many do report that they feel an incredible sense of accomplishment. They feel empowered. Taking risks has paid off in the most meaningful way imaginable: a better life for them and their family.

You should feel proud of yourself for going after what you wanted. You had a vision, you pursued it and now you're living it (or soon you will be)! And don't let anyone tell you otherwise.

Many women who work flexible hours talk about receiving condescending comments, such as: "How lucky you are that your company lets you do it" or "How fortunate that you have the kind of job that allows you to work those hours." This is pure nonsense. Negotiating a flexible work arrangement has nothing to do with luck and everything to do with believing in yourself, having a plan and following your dream. Whatever you do, don't downplay your success. Celebrate it. Not only did you take charge of your own life, but you are also a pioneer paving the way for other women to follow in your footsteps.

There are times now when I almost feel guilty that my life is so great – as if having a good life is something to feel bad about. I rarely experience burnout or a sense of being stretched in a million directions like I once did. For the most part, I feel energized. I have managed to achieve what feels to me like the right mix of work time and Zachary time, and the things I have given up to do it don't seem all that important anymore.

Through my many discussions with women, I have come to realize that the tremendous benefits of creating your own flexible work arrangement go far beyond blending work and motherhood. There are also the benefits of learning to manage your time better, taking charge of your life and living in the moment. Essentially, the journey to flexible work teaches us a lot about ourselves and results in positive shifts in how we think and approach our day-to-day lives. This chapter will celebrate your journey and the benefits you are about to enjoy.

Realizing you control your own happiness

Women who successfully make the transition to a more flexible work arrangement experience a very powerful sense of control over their destiny. Not surprisingly, taking a risk to get what they want instills a sense of confidence in their ability to design their own lives. For many women this is a revelation. They realize – often for the first time in their adult lives – that they do in fact have some control over their own happiness.

Donna, the public affairs professional who traded in her job with a health care institution to start her own business and spend more time with her daughter, talks with great enthusiasm about her new life. She says it taught her a lot about herself. "I didn't know until I left my job to work on my own that my life could be so much better," says Donna. "I've made changes that haven't been the end of the world. In fact, making the decision to leave made me realize I could make any decision after that. The other day I turned to my husband and said, 'Oh my God, can you believe we have this life?'"

Women who successfully make the transition to flexible work experience a very powerful sense of control over their destiny.

Pay attention to this new and sometimes euphoric feeling of being in control of your destiny. You can simply revel in it or you can stretch it further by applying it to other areas of your life. You've already proven to yourself that you can make decisions that are right for you – so don't stop there. Maybe there are other things you've been dreaming of doing, such as going back to school, moving to a different city or submitting a story you wrote to the local newspaper. Go after these dreams and ambitions whenever you can. Take the confidence you've gained and feed it by taking more risks. This is an almost surefire way of continuing to build the life you want.

When I realized that I could work fewer hours and still have a thriving business, I gave in to Vince's suggestion that we take a month off last summer. While the idea of making no money and doing no new business development for a whole month frightened me at first, I encouraged myself to have confidence that it would work out in the end. And it did! It was a wonderful month and I could see how relaxed the whole family was as a result of it. Achieving a better balance between work and Zachary has also been an important catalyst for writing this book. Besides the fact that I really wanted to share with other women my enthusiasm about flexible work, I also realized that if I could live this vision, then there was nothing stopping me from writing a book about it!

Take a moment to think about what you have achieved for yourself and your family through your new flexible work arrangement. If you haven't realized it already, you'll see that you have been responsible for going after a dream and making it real. And if you can make this dream come true, then what's stopping you from going after your other dreams?

Learning to live in the moment

Shifting to flexible work gives many women more time with their children and more opportunities to turn work off. This break from a normally harried existence is often just what women need to live in the moment. Think about it. Kids are all about living in the moment. They don't dwell on the past or worry about the future. They are interested in what is happening right now, this very instant. As adults we often lose the ability to be in the moment because we're always thinking about what's next on our "to do" list, including how we're going to solve a problem that's just presented itself. We even worry about stuff that may never happen. And the busier we are, the more difficult it seems to slow down. Many women say that one of the greatest benefits to flexible work is relearning to stop and smell the roses.

Suzy, the communications consultant and mother of two, attributes a reduction in stress to her move to a more flexible work arrangement. She made the shift from working full time with a communications firm to consulting out of her home four days a week. "I really do appreciate life with so much more depth," says Suzy. "For the first time in so long I saw the fall. I feel closer to nature. Relationships are more meaningful. I really am living in the moment. I haven't lived in the moment since I was a kid."

Another wonderful outcome of focusing on the present and enjoying your children is that you begin to take life a little less seriously. Playing dress-up or making Play-Doh animals forces you to use your imagination, which can be lots of fun. Many women find that the more playtime they actually get with their children, the more that playfulness crosses into their work life. Some women even feel it gives them a creative edge they didn't have before because now they're not solely, intensely focused on work all the time.

Betty, the insurance agency analyst who changed positions to work part time after the birth of her daughter, says that working flexible hours has changed her perspective on life. "Children give you an excuse to be goofy," she says. "I used to be a real perfectionist. If I made a mistake or copied down a phone message incorrectly I got stirred up about it. I definitely do not take myself as seriously as I used to. Now I think that life's too short for sweating the small stuff."

It may take a few months or even a year of working flexible hours before you can really appreciate the change in how you are seeing and experiencing life. But when you do, you'll never want it any other way!

Happy moms make happy families

Many women working flexible hours share a common philosophy: They are doing something that they believe is not only right for them, but for the whole family. Many mothers have confided in me that while they still question whether they are spending enough time with their children, they believe that blending work and motherhood makes them happier individuals. Being happier, women say, makes them better, more patient mothers and wives, and creates a more positive home environment for the whole family.

Susan, the mother who traded in her full-time job for a three-day-a-week position with far less responsibility, reports feeling much more relaxed and less rushed. Susan felt that the stress of working full time was spilling over into her family and social life. In fact, she felt so stressed that she started worrying about her health. “People tell me I look more relaxed, so it must be outwardly noticeable,” says Susan. “I'm also interacting better with my family. I think my husband would say he's noticed a difference. The experience has really taught me to be more assertive about the balance in my life.”

When we work flexible hours, we are also sending an important message to our children.

When we work flexible hours, we are also sending an important message to our children. We're saying that they're important, but work is too. This is probably the biggest reason that women talk so enthusiastically about their flexible work arrangements. They are thrilled that they have managed to balance two things that are so very important to them. And if we know that even young babies are affected by their mother's moods, then happy moms are bound to create happy households.

Monika, the single mother who left a comptroller position with a mid-sized company to run her own accounting practice, is confident that this move has brought her closer to her daughters. Working fewer hours and a more flexible schedule has made it possible to carve out more quality time with her girls. "Before I started working for myself, dinner was always a rush," she says. "At night we were literally at each other's throats. And in the mornings I was always telling them that they were going to make me late for work. We had all the material things we wanted, but we had no family life. Since I started working for myself, money has become less important. It comes down to quality of life versus the toys. So even though there have been times where scraping together five dollars for milk was difficult, we've spent summers together playing on our front lawn and having a great time."

Of course I'm not suggesting that a flexible work arrangement is the secret to every woman's happiness. But for women looking for a better balance between work and motherhood, it sure seems to be a good start.

Flexible work can be fulfilling

One of the most important questions that women ask themselves when they consider a move to a flexible work situation is: Can I do this and still have a satisfying career? For most women the answer is yes. While women readily acknowledge that they are knowingly slowing down their careers or giving up job opportunities to work flexible hours, they are nonetheless enthusiastic about the work they do. They still have a sense that what they are doing is meaningful and important. Whether it's the interaction with other adults, the satisfaction of a job well done or the feelings of self-worth that come from being paid for what they do, women in flexible arrangements really do experience fulfillment.

Carolyn, the mother of three who negotiated to work full time during her firm's busy season and three days a week the rest of the year, is a perfect example. Despite working reduced hours for nearly ten years at a major accounting firm, she has experienced a tremendous amount of career growth. Even after switching to flexible hours, Carolyn made partner in the firm and continues to be offered new and exciting career opportunities. Today she is the national director of human resources. "Sometimes I look back and say how did I get here?" says Carolyn. "I'm surprised that I'm a partner – with three kids and flex hours. I did have to cut out training and travel, and at times raise my hand and say I'm in way over my head. But I was also a good time manager and I had a goal: I wanted to be with my kids."

Making partner on a reduced work schedule is not the norm in most companies, but lots of women working flexible hours still feel good about the work they do and derive other important benefits from their new arrangements. Margo, a graphic designer and mother of Leland, five, and Sonia, two and a half, has found that working as little as two days a week helps her stay up to date with trends and keep her design skills tuned. Wanting more time with her children, Margo traded in her four-day-a-week position in the graphic design department of a financial institution to work as a freelancer two days a week. "I'm not in it to make beautiful pictures," says Margo. "I'm in it to keep my hands in it. The money is secondary to the notion that I can still be a designer. I haven't lost my edge. I find I learn something from every project I get. And the best part is that I'm not flying out of here every day to pick up my kids from day care."

Successfully designing your own work schedule to give you more time with your children makes the end result more satisfying. While I have given up on growing our business for the time being, I continue to be challenged by my work and really enjoy interacting with and helping my clients. And that suits me just fine if it means that I also get to spend mornings dipping my toes in a nearby creek with Zachary.

You may never want to go back

Women in flexible work arrangements are often surprised to realize they never really want to go back to a full-time job or career. We all seem to start off thinking that working flexible hours is a temporary arrangement to help us be around when our children are babies, toddlers or preschoolers. But once we get into flexible work and all the other benefits it brings, many of us can't see returning to the way we worked in the past. I think what also dawns on us is the fact that just because our children start going to school doesn't mean they don't need us and that we don't need them. This motivates women to keep readjusting their work schedules to suit the changing needs of their children and families.

Dana, the journalist who switched from full time to part time, found that her children actually needed her more once they started going to school. Dana worked full time while Stewart, eight, and daughter, Grace, five, were young. It wasn't until her son entered first grade and started having difficulty that she realized she needed and wanted to be around more. She began by taking a four-month leave of absence, but at the end of the four months she knew she couldn't go back full time. So she negotiated a part-time position with her employer and doesn't have any plans to change her arrangement any time soon.

"After I started working part time I noticed the huge benefits for my children," says Dana. "My son loved the fact that I picked him up every day from school. He relaxed when he realized he wasn't out there on his own. I feel like I have more time to focus on the children and their needs. I feel closer to them and more tuned in to what's going on in their lives. I can't really picture any point when this goes away."

It's exciting to discover that a flexible work arrangement really can give you the best of both worlds. So it's not surprising that women get inspired by the prospect of working this way for a while, or even for the rest of their lives. That's probably the single greatest benefit to taking the plunge into the flexible work world: You may just find that it's too good to give up – ever.

Final words of wisdom from women who've been there

Women who have successfully made the transition to flexible work have these final words of wisdom to pass on to others pursuing a more balanced life:

Don't neglect yourself

Of course this statement applies to all women, not just those with flexible work schedules. But some women working flexible hours have found that juggling work and their role as a hands-on mom leaves them feeling like that's all they do. They report that they often end up devoting every minute to their work and their children. They talk about giving up time with friends, workouts or simply reading a good book. While these things are bound to be challenged when you have children, setting aside no time for yourself is a threat to your flexible work arrangement.

You need some time to stay in touch with your feelings about how things are going. Otherwise, you're likely to burn out quickly and reduce your chances of long-term success. So if you are committed to making it work, do yourself a favor and schedule time for yourself. It will go a long way in helping you appreciate and enjoy the life you've created for yourself and your family.

Scheduling time for yourself will go a long way in helping you appreciate and enjoy the life you've created.

Take time with your partner

In the same way women readily give up time for themselves, they also have a tendency to put time with their partners on the back burner when the focus is on work and children. Staying connected to your partner is not only crucial to your long-term relationship; it is essential to the success of your flexible work arrangement. While you may see the arrangement as "your thing," it probably wouldn't work as well or even at all without the support of your partner. To ensure that your partner continues to be supportive of your new flexible hours, you have to communicate with each other on a regular basis. Take some time together outside of your parenting and work responsibilities. It's important to make sure you both feel good about the choices you've made.

Keep visioning

Many people believe that once they've successfully negotiated a flexible work arrangement, the need to work on a vision and plan simply ends. This is a big mistake. As life ebbs and flows, so do your needs and the needs of your family. It's so important to keep going back to your vision, and reviewing and revising it to suit your ever-changing life (use the visioning exercise on page 149 to help you). Reviewing your vision is also an important way to make sure you and your husband stay on the same wavelength. Vince and I schedule time each year to work on our vision, both for our business and personal life. It brings us closer as a couple and ensures that major life decisions are made consciously and together.

Spread the word

Many women feel completely alone and out in left field when they're trying to go after a flexible work arrangement. Resources such as this book aren't always enough. Women still want to talk with other women who've been down the same road. That's where you come in. You've gone the distance and know what it takes to create a vision for yourself and make it a reality. Share your story and your experiences with other women contemplating a similar transition. As you probably know all too well, it's hard to do it on your own. Your support alone could make all the difference in a woman's life.

Enjoy every minute

Like anything in life, it's easy to get caught up in the day-to-day trials and tribulations of a flexible work arrangement. Don't let this happen. You've worked too hard not to enjoy every minute of your new life. Don't question it, just live it!

On with the journey

Well, there you have it – everything I know and have learned from other women about flexible work and how to create an arrangement that is right for you. For me the journey has been at times crazy and at other times better than I ever could have imagined. In the end, making the shift to flexible work has been the most rewarding decision I have ever made for myself and my family. I am now the proud mother of two children: Zachary, nearly four, and his new little brother, Ethan, six months. So the juggling is even more complicated, but I am once again reminded of all the wonderful, magical moments that motherhood brings. And I don't plan to miss a thing.

AFTERWORD

Flexing with Your Partner

As someone who has enjoyed the tremendous benefits of "flexing" with my husband for the last three years, I couldn't end this book without introducing you to the possibility of two-parent flexing. Why not consider having your partner switch to a flexible arrangement, too?

While far more women than men are arranging or working flexible hours, many husbands and partners yearn for a piece of the action, too. And why not? If you've got a good thing going, why not make it even better? For many couples, when both parents work some kind of flexible schedule, it takes the pressure off one parent to always be the primary income earner or the primary child-care provider. Each of them can play a more active parenting role by working fewer hours.

For many couples this feels even riskier than having only one parent switching to flexible hours. Often there is a great sense of income security as long as one person stays on the full-time career track. But the couples who flex together enjoy double the flexibility. And while both may lose income by cutting back, they usually spend far less or nothing at all on child care. Many couples who work flex hours also feel that there is less chance for resentment in the relationship, since neither person is putting his or her career on the line more than the other. And they are better able to manage the changing needs of their children when they have the flexibility to help each other out.

"By having two people flex, you each flex less and both get the benefits," says Jessica DeGroot, a mother of two children and founder of the Third Path Institute (www.thirdpath.org), a nonprofit project that works to assist families and individuals in balancing work and home life. "When you bring fathers into the solution, it's not just child care, it's a parent. It also means you're thinking of your husband as a partner and not just someone who is supporting your own goals." Jessica knows intimately the benefit of having a flex partner: She has been sharing the care of her children with her husband, Jeff, for more than ten years. Each has adjusted his or her work schedule over time to ensure that one of them was always home with the children. "Jeff and I feel very connected because of the shared care," says Jessica. "There's no guilt or resentment. We're both more focused on our common goal of raising our children, and we're both moving forward in developing our careers. It has been very positive for our relationship."

By having two people flex, you each flex less and both get the benefits.

Andrea and her husband, computer system administrators for different companies, decided to both work flexible hours to keep their firstborn out of day care. They negotiated sharing the same job at Andrea's company, a bank, before Andrea went on maternity leave. After their daughter, Savannah, was born, they both began working three days a week at the bank, with one day overlapping so they can bring each other up to speed on work issues. As a result, Savannah spends one day a week with her grandparents and the rest of the time with one of her parents. While Andrea readily acknowledges the challenges in getting used to their new arrangement, after several months she feels like it's finally starting to work for them. "We always knew we wanted one of us to stay home with our children," says Andrea. "But our relationship was important to us, too, so we didn't want to work different shifts. And because we are in a constantly changing field, we felt that we both needed to work to stay on top of the rapid changes in our industry."

It may be too soon for you to even start thinking about involving your husband as a flexible partner. Or you may decide that this is not right for you. Don't rule it out completely, however. Getting your husband to join in, too, is one more potential benefit of your successful arrangement. If it has made you a happier person, it might do the same for him. The potential positive results for your relationship and your family are numerous.

Keep in mind that it often takes time for men to realize how much their wives are enjoying flexible work. And many men need encouragement to explore their feelings about it and connect to what they really want. "It is as scary for a man to think about asking for a flexible work arrangement as it was for the first woman who put her child in day care to go back to work," says Jessica. "I know women are usually the catalyst for the change, but that doesn't mean that men can't benefit, too. Something very powerful happens when we start thinking about it as not just a woman's issue."

Visioning Exercise

Set aside at least 30 to 45 minutes to go through this visioning exercise. Grab a cup of tea or coffee, and a notepad and pen. Go to a quiet room where you can close the door and really think without interruption. Then begin envisioning what an ideal week would look like under your new flexible work arrangement. Work your way through the following questions:

1. What kind of child care do you have in place?
   Who is taking care of your child?
   - Do you drop off your child at a day-care center with other children and lots of colorful arts and crafts on the walls?
   - Do you have a babysitter coming into your home and playing with your child in your family room?
   - Are you bringing your child to your mother's home?
   - Have you found a mother in the neighborhood who already takes two or three children into her home?
   - Do you see yourself as the primary caregiver, with an occasional babysitter covering for you when you have to leave the house for meetings?

   How many days a week is your child in care?
   - Is it three full days from 8:30 a.m. to 5:30 p.m.?
   - Is it five mornings a week from 8:30 a.m. to 12:30 p.m.?

- Does it change from week to week with the ebb and flow of your work?

2. What kind of support do you anticipate getting from your partner?
   - Does he pick up your children or drop them off at day care on certain days of the week?
   - Does he take over at home at 6:00 p.m. three nights a week so that you can work at night?
   - Does he get your children ready in the morning so you can get to the office early and finish early?
   - Does he take the odd day off when the kids are sick or you have to put in an unscheduled workday?
3. How many days a week do you work and for how many hours? (Think about your children's schedules when you answer this question.)
   - Do you cram full-time work hours into four longer days? If so, can you live with not seeing your children four days a week?
   - Do you work a three-day week with two days a week off?
   - Do you spread part-time hours over five days so you can be with your new baby every afternoon or morning?
   - Do you work a four-day week – two days in the office and two at home – so you can be closer to your child even when you are working?
4. How do you see your actual workweek unfolding? When do you start work and what time do you finish? List all the things you envision yourself doing with your children and then look at what kind of work schedule might accommodate that list.

- Do you work at home when your baby is asleep (during naps and at night)?
- Do you start work at 8:30 a.m. after your children have gone to school and then quit at 3:30 p.m. when they arrive home?
- Do you go into the office at 7:30 a.m. so you can leave at 4:00 p.m.?
- Do you work mornings and then spend afternoons with your children?

5. What kind of physical work environment do you see around you? Do you work at home, in the office or a bit of both?
   - Do you work out of a spare room in your house, wearing a pair of jeans and snacking on cookies from your kitchen?
   - Do you work in an office where you're constantly surrounded by and being interrupted by colleagues?
   - Do you attend meetings in the office on specific days and work the rest of the time in your home office?
6. What kind of flexible work arrangement (working for yourself, job sharing, etc.) might suit your job and your skills?
   - Could your position be split up into a job-sharing arrangement? Do you have a potential job-sharing partner in mind?
   - Are you the kind of person who could work independently from home? Could your particular job be done from home?
   - Could you turn your skills and expertise into a viable small business?
   - Could parts of your job easily be handled by another staff person, such as an administrative assistant or coordinator?

- Do you need to be in the office to manage staff and team projects?

7. What level of responsibility do you have within your new flexible work arrangement?
   - Are you still managing ten people and six projects or do you have less responsibility than before?
   - Is it realistic to think you can manage staff and be responsible for their performance appraisals if you're only in the office three days a week?
   - Can you manage a budget if you will not be in the office to approve all expenditures?
   - Do you still take on the same number of assignments as you did before shifting to a more flexible work arrangement?
   - Which responsibilities could you hand over to accommodate your new schedule and work arrangement?
8. How much time do you spend each day commuting to and from work?
   - Are you prepared to drive long distances for the right job and flexible work arrangement?
   - Are you willing to commute 15 to 20 minutes so you can be closer to home and your children if they need you?
   - Do you want to get rid of your commute altogether and work from home?
9. Do you picture working at the same kind of job you did before or are you doing something new?
   - Could you restructure your current job into the kind of flexible work arrangement you're looking for? Would your company support you?

- Are you excited about the prospect of starting your own business?
- Since your priorities have changed, do you have a new line of work or type of company in mind?

10. Now comes the reality check. You've got your vision and you need to figure out how you can afford it. You may need to work through this question separately since you will have to spend time gathering information.
    - Start by working out your new monthly household income (add your new projected income to your spouse's existing income) to see exactly how much money will be coming in.
    - Now list all your existing monthly expenses (if you've never tracked these you may have to go back to credit card bills and bank statements to build a spending picture). Add in the cost of the child care you envision in your flexible work arrangement. Also, make sure to factor in any monthly savings you will realize from your new work schedule (such as reduced gas and car maintenance costs, or fewer bought lunches and work clothes).
    - Compare the projected money coming in versus the projected money going out. Unless you've been living well below your means until now (which few people do), you will likely have to look for expenses that you can cut back in order to make your vision a reality.
    - Can you get rid of a car or trade one in for a second-hand vehicle?
    - Can you reduce your monthly food or phone bills?
    - Can you save money by buying children's clothing and toys at a second-hand store?

- Can you renegotiate your mortgage for a longer term to reduce the payments? Can you move to a less expensive house?
- You may find that you simply can't come up with a way to cut enough expenses. If this is the case, you'll need to go back to the drawing board and tweak your vision into something your family can afford to live with.

How to Write a Winning Proposal

Include the essentials in your introduction

- Outline the kind of flexible work arrangement you're proposing: four-day workweek, job sharing, etc.
- Show examples of how you will continue to be a valuable employee.
- List benefits to the company, such as cost savings and keeping a valuable employee.
- State why you're proposing this: for a better work/family balance.
- Show how your proposal fits in with company policy or mission, if applicable.
- Demonstrate how flexible work can be good for both you and your employer (include key points that you've found in the studies that support flex work arrangements).
- Make it clear that this is a draft for review and discussion.

Outline your proposed work arrangement

- What is the actual schedule you're proposing?
    - how many hours per week you'd like to work
    - which days you plan to work

    - how you'll deal with peak periods of your business and key meetings on days off
    - how your key responsibilities fit into this new schedule
- Where do you plan to work?
    - if in the office, think about whether you need the same setup you have now or could get by with sharing an office or computer
    - if from home, describe your setup, technology, the child care you have in place, etc.
- How will your job responsibilities be redefined?
    - what you will be responsible for
    - what should be reassigned and to whom, or to what kind of position

Show how you will remain accessible

- How will you ensure that you connect regularly with coworkers and your boss about projects, progress reports, etc.?
- Suggest ways to be available on your days off, when required (by e-mail, cell phone, scheduled calls, etc.).
- How will you handle emergency requests and work periods when overtime is required to meet a deadline?

Describe how you will make this work

- Remind your boss that you have demonstrated the skills (self-discipline, productivity, success with deadlines, etc.) that suit a flexible work arrangement.
- Describe how you'll continue to work closely with team members under your new schedule.
- Show how you'll meet deadlines.
- Talk about how you'll resolve conflicts that arise.

Paint your new financial picture

- Include the salary you are proposing (i.e., three days a week = 65 percent of original salary) and explain why it makes sense.
- Indicate what kind of benefits package you are hoping for: full benefits, prorated benefits adjusted to the reduced number of hours you will be working, half the cost of your plan, etc.
- How many vacation days and sick days do you propose? Adjust your current allocation to reflect the number of days you will be working in the new arrangement. If you were entitled to three weeks and will now be working a three-day week, you would be entitled to three weeks times three days – or nine days.
- Make sure you indicate all cost savings to your employer.

Recommend regular performance reviews

- Suggest regular (i.e., quarterly) meetings to review how the new arrangement is going.
- List specific criteria or goals that should be reviewed at each meeting, such as your ability to meet deadlines, achieve a sales target or land a certain number of new clients.
- Recommend ways that you or your boss could solicit and evaluate feedback from your coworkers or clients.

Include proof that flexible hours work

- Start with examples of successful flexible work arrangements within your company if they exist. Include a bit about the employee's role, the actual flexible work arrangement and testimonials from the relevant manager about how the arrangement is working out.

- Include a summary of the research you have found in support of flexible work arrangements in general, and if possible the specific kind of arrangement you are proposing. Backup articles and statistics are good to have, but don't include entire studies in your proposal, just the highlights.

Wrap it up with a summary

- Remind your employer why you think you are suited to a flexible work arrangement. Reiterate your track record with the company: your accomplishments, longevity, etc.
- Explain why you think this proposed arrangement will work for you (increased job satisfaction) and for the company (more cost-effective and the chance to keep a good employee).

Acknowledgements

I can hardly believe that after three years this book is now a reality. I have many people to thank for helping me get here. I am most grateful to the many women willing to speak with me about their own transitions to flexible work. You inspired me, and your stories will offer many mothers valuable insights into the work/family dilemma. I also received wisdom from the following people: Jessica DeGroot from the Third Path Institute, Jim Freer and Wendy Hirschberg at Ernst & Young, Pat Brown at First Tennessee Bank, and Pat Katepoo of Work Options.

I am honored to have Sally Armstrong kick off the book with her seasoned perspective on women's issues. And I was fortunate to find my editor, June Rogers, who edited around my ever-changing flexible schedule.

I have been blown away by the many people who donated their time and expertise to this project, including my test readers (all busy moms who made time to read and critique the book), copy editor Kathy Martin O'Neil, cover photographer Peter Bregg, and cover design team Emmanuel Papadakis and Maria Gaspar.

Friends who have been subjected to my incessant desire to explore the issues around flexible work have been patient and encouraging. Rosemary and James, you never doubted that this book would happen and you helped make it so. Suzanne, Jenny, Suzy, Tiffany, and my sister-in-law Susan, thanks for your contributions and for listening a lot.

A note to my family: I know you didn't always understand why I was writing this book, but as always you supported me nonetheless. And Mom, thanks for consistently making me feel like what I have to say is worth listening to – I hope you're right.

Of course, if it weren't for my husband, Vince, no words would ever have been put on paper. Your put-your-money-where-your-mouth-is mantra has served me well on many occasions. Thank you for sacrificing some of your own goals for mine.

For more than a decade I have been haunted by the words of the late Keitha McLean, who once encouraged me to "continue to stretch with my writing and then stretch some more." I guess your words finally sunk in.

About Jacqueline Foley

Jacqueline Foley is an accomplished writer whose works have appeared in *Homemaker's* and *Canadian Living* magazines. Jacqueline is also a regular contributor to the Work and Money section of Mocha Sofa (www.mochasofa.ca), a website for women. *Flex Appeal* is her first book.

Jacqueline works three days a week out of her home in a firm that does strategic consulting for charities. She is married (her husband Vince is also her business partner) and is the mother of two boys, Zachary, nearly four, and Ethan, six months. She lives in Stouffville, a small town just outside of Toronto, Ontario.

If you have questions about flexible work or want to share a story about achieving work/family balance, you can e-mail Jacqueline at jacqueline@getflexappeal.com.

Empower Other Mothers – Share Your Story

While writing this book I learned that women really do love to share their stories and that these stories can be very empowering. Seeing that other women have been successful at achieving work/family balance through flexible work is a powerful motivator for mothers seeking a better balance. Women also find it comforting to see that they are not alone in facing the challenges that come with juggling work and kids.

That's why I encourage you to share your story or your own work/family dilemma with other women through our website. You have the power to help women face their fears and go after the life they want.

Write to me at:
jacqueline@getflexappeal.com

Or visit our website:
www.getflexappeal.com